**Being
Number One:
Rebuilding
the U.S. Economy**

Being Number One: Rebuilding the U.S. Economy

Gail Garfield Schwartz
Pat Choate

LexingtonBooks
D.C. Heath and Company
Lexington, Massachusetts
Toronto

Library of Congress Cataloging in Publication Data

Schwartz, Gail Garfield.
  Being number one: rebuilding the U.S. economy.

  Bibliography: p.
  Includes index.
    1. United States—Economic policy—1971- I. Choate, Pat, joint
author. II. Title.
HC106.7.S3636   338.973   80-8604
ISBN 0-669-04308-7

Copyright © 1980 by D.C. Heath and Company

Published simultaneously in Canada

Printed in the United States of America

International Standard Book Number: 0-669-04308-7

Library of Congress Catalog Card Number: 80-8604

*To Ralph R. Widner,
president of the Academy
for Contemporary Problems,
in recognition of his
outstanding contribution
to economic development*

Contents

List of Figures

List of Tables

Acknowledgments

Many individuals have reviewed drafts of this book. They include corporate leaders, government officials, labor-union representatives, economists, and political scientists. To list them would take advantage of their helpfulness and candor; but we are very grateful to all for their many contributions.

We are grateful, also, to the Academy for Contemporary Problems, Columbus, Ohio, and Washington, D.C., for support of our paper, "Revitalizing the U.S. Economy: A Brief for National Sectoral Policies." Its publication by the Academy in January 1980 encouraged us to complete this book.

Unless otherwise indicated, the sources of statistics are the *Statistical Abstract of the United States,* 100th edition, 1979, published by the U.S. Bureau of the Census, and the *1980 U.S. Industrial Outlook,* published by the U.S. Department of Commerce. We thank various government agencies for providing unpublished data and calculations.

We appreciate most the encouragement of our respective spouses, Lester J. Schwartz and Diane C. Choate.

If there are any errors of fact or interpretation in this book, the authors bear sole responsibility.

**Being
Number One:
Rebuilding
the U.S. Economy**

1 Introduction

If the United States is to reverse the present downward spiral in its standard of living, a national economic development strategy is essential. This strategy must recognize the reality that our economic woes are not temporary and are not responsive to the incoherent and self-defeating practices now presented as national policy.

Inflation and high unemployment have been with us for the better part of a decade. The changes in inflation rates and unemployment rates have been a matter of degree, not of substance. Even in the growth periods of this decade, unemployment remained high; even in the slack periods, inflation rates stayed up.

The cause of stagflation is simple. American industrial productivity is falling and our products are not competitive in world and domestic markets. In steel, autos, textiles, aluminum, electronics, machine tools, and many other categories, American firms fail to produce the right goods of sufficient quality and quantity at competitive prices.

Corporate management, labor, and government all bear some responsibility for the relative decline of U.S. productivity and output. While management may be slow to innovate, as in the auto industry, or lax in quality control, as in the electronics industry, labor has resisted new technologies in fear they would drive jobs away. Government policies have constrained corporations in a highly competitive world market. Antitrust laws, environmental laws, health, safety, and product-standard regulations have placed heavy burdens on firms. Although most of these government policies may address desirable objectives, they are administered without due regard for their counterproductive impacts on cost structures and, hence, on our national prosperity.

By contrast, the nations that are aggressively competing with the U.S. have developed national economic-development strategies that involve joint action by business, labor, and government. The United States must do the same.

The United States faces many domestic challenges in the 1980s: the revitalization of our urban areas, an adjustment to renewed rural growth, persistent structural unemployment, growing demands on the social security system, and the creation of millions of new jobs for our increasing work force. But the present condition of the U.S. economy raises disturbing ques-

1

tions about our ability to respond to these imperatives and, simultaneously, provokes doubts about the nation's future economic and social stability. Our success or failure in dealing with the economy will profoundly affect our international political position. Moreover, it is simply unrealistic to pretend that we can maintain our national defenses unless the United States is a dominant economic power.

The United States is still the largest national market in the world. It still has the largest civilian labor force of any advanced industrial nation. It still has the most productive economy, overall, in the world, and it still has the largest national product of any single nation. If the United States is to maintain its high standard of living, make further strides toward a more equitable distribution of income, further improve the quality of life for all, and encourage a more stable world political environment, its economy must grow.

Being number one—the dominant world economic power—does not mean that the United States seeks to thrive at the expense of other nations. Economic growth in the United States will complement the economic-development efforts of both the mature and developing nations. Improving the quality of and maintaining competitive prices for American goods sold abroad will benefit the buyers as well as the sellers. At the same time, expanding purchasing power of American corporate and individual consumers will allow them to buy the specialties of other nations. "A rising tide raises all boats" is as true in the international as in the national context.

But the U.S. economy is too complex for strategies that focus on single industries. Many industries are linked in an interdependent chain or sector. For example, when sales of domestic automobiles slump, that causes a decline in production of tires, upholstery, seatbelts, batteries, and plastic, aluminum, and steel parts.

Because each sector has its own particular cost structure and its own market conditions, efforts to improve the performance of American firms should deal with the specific concerns of each sector. Through sector-specific strategies, we can enhance efficiency while promoting other national goals, such as economic equality and conservation of resources.

Sectoral strategies are needed for declining sectors, mature sectors, and emerging and high-growth sectors, which also face stiff competition. The semiconductor industry, the telecommunications industry, the biochemical sector, and other high-technology manufacturing and service activities can provide many jobs in the future for both assembly workers and skilled technicians. Other nations have already recognized the importance of these emerging industries and are engaged in major public-private campaigns to expand production, accelerate research, and train workers for new tasks. To meet the major economic challenges for the rest of the twentieth century and beyond, the United States must immediately create a new logic for public interventions in the economy. Business management must demonstrate a long-range concern for the viability of domestic industries. Labor must become more sensitive to the competitive consequences of its actions.

The Economic Chain

Operationally, the U.S. economy is a manufacturing and service network of hundreds of economic activities. Many such activities are linked in a chain of interdependence. These linked industries constitute sectors that are smaller and more discrete than the major divisions of the economy or macro sectors, for example, agriculture, mining, manufacturing, services, and trade. These linked industries themselves cross macro sectors—as in the utilization of agricultural byproducts for manufacturing purposes or computers for teleservices.

The manufacturing macro sector in the United States has been declining relative to the entire economy. In part this is a result of economic maturation—the move into what others call the service economy or the postindustrial economy. In part, however, this relative decline reflects absolute declines in some manufacturing industries, such as steel, bicycles, apparel, textiles, and automobiles. These industries have failed to increase productivity. They are experiencing growing competition from foreign producers. Some of them, such as the steel industry, have already entered the crisis phase that has occasioned government's protectionist measures and adjustment assistance. These government policies, however, have not always helped to strengthen the industries in terms of output or market share.

Other industries stand threatened by similar dislocations. Not all of the industries at risk are mature. Many, such as biochemicals and laser systems, are at the cutting edge of future technologies and are the growth industries of tomorrow.

Certain service sectors are also vital for future economic development. A complex domestic economy needs many business services. Moreover, the United States exports many services, such as engineering, technical consulting, and communications, which helps to balance international payments and to provide high-paying jobs for Americans at home. Although these services are labor-intensive, these service sectors are only beginning to explore the possiblities for increasing productivity through automated data systems, telecommunications, and other technological or capital-intensive means.

As all countries become increasingly service-oriented, world international competition in these sectors will increase too. If American professionals and technicians are to maintain their marketability at home and abroad, it is not premature to assess the potential advantage for American firms in these sectors and to take steps to improve their productivity and quality of performance.

During the last year, there has been a growing concern about the sluggish performance of the U.S. economy. Various formulas to raise productivity and counter the evident technological weakness of the American economy have been proposed in the press and the Congress. Editorials and news columns have highlighted individual cases of irrational or contradictory government policies that hurt American industry by raising costs or constraining markets. And, of course, when the nation's least-efficient automobile-assembly corporation teetered on the edge of bankruptcy, Congress rushed in with a poorly thought-out, patently inequitable expenditure of dollars to give the Chrysler corporation one more chance.

The United States can ill afford to rush in after the fact with ad hoc measures to save specific plants or firms. This is irrational and inequitable. To avoid such folly we need forward-looking, planned sectoral-development policies. Such policies are not farfetched; they are a workable policy option. We will explain why and how in the ensuing chapters.

Elements of a New Economic Order

The overwhelming fact of the new economic order is that, in all types of economic systems, from capitalistic to communistic, government is an integral part of the economy. In the United States, federal, state, and local expenditures amount to one-third of the gross national product (GNP).[1] These expenditures include not only maintaining the defense establishment, delivering direct services, and collecting taxes, but also a wide range of interventions in the market for money, credit, commodities, goods, and services. The interventions include regulation for social purposes of health, safety, and preservation of the environment. The interventions take many forms, some of which are beneficial and some of which are debilitating from the point of view of increasing the profits and productivity of business. It is doubtful that many forms of intervention in the economy will prove amenable to total retraction, like deregulation of airlines. Government is an essential thread in the intricate web of American capitalism. Government cannot be removed from the marketplace without destroying the entire interdependent system.

The Service Economy

A second characteristic of the new economic order is the large number of advanced industrial—or, as is the more popular phrase, postindustrial—

economies. These economies are characterized by a high level of automation, a high proportion of services, and a high ratio of white-collar to blue-collar workers. The United States, Switzerland, Sweden, the Netherlands, France, the United Kingdom, and the Federal Republic of Germany are the leading representatives of postindustrialization.

While in the poorer industrialized nations, such as Italy, the high proportion of white-collar and service-sector jobs in part reflects governmental alleviation of chronic unemployment through public services, in the richer countries it represents consumer demand in the private sector facilitated by a high standard of living. The large number of nations in this category shows that the United States has no monopoly on service technology.

In a service economy, however, the basic macro sectors—mining, agriculture, and manufacturing—must support the service sectors. A larger and larger nonproducing population can become a drag on the domestic economy if its economic activity does not contribute to productivity increases or to expanding markets outside the United States. The tilt of the economy toward services means that fewer and fewer jobs are truly "essential" to the economy's basic output. This has several consequences in a stagnant or slow-growing economy. For one thing, labor becomes more intransigent and determined to protect jobs and income. This psychology, which cannot be easily demonstrated by statistics, has undoubtedly contributed to the inelasticity of wages even in the face of recession.

Another consequence is that the service sector educates and maintains a reserve pool of nonessential labor ready to assume essential jobs should circumstances force it out of the service sector. The phenomenon of people with Ph.D.s taking jobs as sales clerks and secretaries, not temporarily but for years, illustrates this process. During the recessions of 1969–1970 and 1974–1975, Wall Street brokers drove taxis.

The threat of worker substitution also exists in the manufacturing macro sector itself. It comes from two main sources other than the reserve pool of service-sector workers. One is redundant workers in industries that are declining. The other is the stream of new workers—immigrants to the United States as well as maturing youth.

The prospect of a swelling labor force competing for relatively fewer jobs leads organized labor in the nonservice sectors to be even more protective of its members' rights to work. Because organized labor protects its member workers' rights to available jobs, the reserve labor cannot invade the primary blue-collar sectors in the areas of the country where labor is well organized. But in depression circumstances, nonunionized primary-sector workers would be vulnerable. Workers in managerial and professional levels of the service sector could command lower-paid white-collar jobs quite easily, and probably could usurp blue-collar jobs as well. The specter of a recession so severe as to bring about this process is unthinkable, perhaps, but not incredible.

The Role of Developing Nations

The third characteristic of the new world economic order is the determination of lesser-developed countries to become self-sufficient economically and to gain a larger share of the world's wealth. These nations offer virtually irresistible opportunities for foreign firms operating within their borders, through free land facilities, tax exemption, and other incentives. The exceedingly low cost of labor—as little as 10 percent of that of American labor in some industries—is encouraged or enforced by many foreign governments. Labor in other countries is approaching U.S. labor in output per unit of labor input. Yet, the production costs of labor in Asia, Southern Europe, Ireland, and South and Central America are a small fraction of domestic-labor production costs.

Moreover, the pool of underutilized labor in countries that have as yet not embarked on economic-development strategies to lure foreign firms is enormous. Firms in the advanced industrial nations are assisted by their own national governments to take advantage of these international opportunities. In the United States, tax laws and such organizations as the National Overseas Investment Corporation, which is sponsored by the U.S. government, have enhanced the overseas operations of many domestic firms.

Not for a moment do we mean to imply that this situation is all bad. There are both humanitarian and self-interested reasons why the private sector should participate in raising the standard of living in the poorer nations. Clearly it is advantageous to build the developing countries through private investment, and to encourage their growing self-sufficiency. But overseas investments of U.S. firms should be considered in the light of overall national economic objectives.

The wealthy oil-rich and mineral-rich nations are currently in the strongest economic-development position, because they can afford to fulfill their enormous growth potential. Those that are not constrained by a small labor force can modernize very rapidly and can skip some of the diseconomies historically associated with industrialization. The smaller countries such as Kuwait and Saudi Arabia can solve their labor-force problems with immigrant or "guest" workers. Surplus Asian labor is already building roads, cleaning hotels, and performing other essential jobs in the Middle East. At the same time as they are developing their own economies, resource-rich nations will develop greater interdependencies with their industrialized debtors. These interdependencies will include agreements that ensure a steady flow of resources in exchange for technological expertise and management skills. Such bargains have already been negotiated by France and Japan to protect their oil supplies. As the benefits of their oil income multiply, oil-rich nations will provide growing markets for a wide variety of goods and services—markets that will be opened up on a most-favored-nation basis. The pace at which the resource-rich countries will develop their manufacturing bases and service bases will vary with a number of considerations, but it is certain that these countries will not be content with low-level technologies.

The immediate consequences for the American economy are not good. New occupations in higher or different technologies may in the aggregate substitute for production jobs "exported" through overseas production by American firms, or for jobs lost by virtue of the competition of imports from firms in low-cost countries. But these occupations can seldom be filled, at least not without extensive retraining, by those whose initial jobs have been affected; they don't require the same skills, and they are likely not to be located in the same place. Thus the pursuit of worldwide economic efficiency and the attainment of domestic economic equity seem to be goals in conflict.

The dislocations caused within the United States by continuing shifts in the world market situation will not soon change. For the foreseeable future, producers can operate mobile workshops, training labor to do simple tasks in country A, and, when prices and wages rise there, can move the operation to an even less-developed country B. Sometimes tasks are repatriated to the United States when the production runs are large enough to permit automation or more capital-intensive production systems. The point is, however, that worldwide mobile workshops will not be eliminated until the gaps between domestic and overseas productivity are reduced and until the opportunities for higher net returns to capital overseas are more carefully controlled.

Sophisticated Leadership

Another characteristic of the new economic order is the quality of its leadership. The younger generation is politically and economically astute. Education for management and the political survival of the fittest have bred unique skills. In Japan, only the best students are given the honor of entering the government, there to manage the public side of Japan's extraordinary public-private economic partnership. German technocrats and scientific managers look for efficiency, productivity, market expansion, and stability in the conduct of public- and private-sector activities. Even in the lesser-developed countries, the sophistication of business leaders is increasing rapidly as more and more of the newly created middle class is becoming educated in the United States, Great Britain, and France. A quantum jump in the quality of economic and political leadership is occurring in both the government of developing nations and in their business enterprises.

Harmonizing Corporate and Public Strategies

Another feature of the new economic order, closely related to scientific management, is the relationship of corporate and government planning. Many key firms in the United States have recently expanded their corporate-planning divisions. But government and business policymakers do not generally act in concert at the strategic stage.

In Europe, where public planning is a long-honored tradition, it is inter-meshed with corporate planning. In France, regional-development pro-grams and industrial policies have been integrated through a network involv-ing the Ministry for Industrial and Scientific Development, the General Plan Commissariat, and the Delegation for Territorial and Regional Man-agement (DATAR), which prepares and implements approved public plans after coordinating them with corporate plans.

European members of the Organization for Economic Cooperation and Development (OECD), the economic fraternity whose interests are inextric-ably linked with those of the United States, have recognized the need to harmonize the many aspects of economic policy and have begun to con-struct the mechanisms to do so. The symbiotic relationship between Japa-nese business and government is the extreme illustration of these mecha-nisms. It poses a challenge to American ingenuity that we have so far failed to meet.

Recognition that the mutual interests of labor and management often outweigh the conflicts between them is emerging in the advanced industrial nations. Germany and the Scandinavian countries are particularly notable for cooperation between labor and management. West Germany's worker-participation tradition dates to the 1920s and was codified with the encour-agement of the United States after World War II. Workers sit on the boards of directors and participate in decisions that in this country are usually the exclusive domain of management—decisions such as scheduling and product design. Codetermination exists on a parity basis in the coal and steel industry and on a one-third basis in other industries. Although the sys-tem is not perfect in the eyes of labor or management, it is working.

West Germany and Japan demonstrate ways of meeting both economic and social objectives in a capitalistic framework without the polarities and traumas now associated with the cyclical behavior and adversary approaches traditional in the United States. They contrast sharply with countries where the adversary approach has reached extremes, such as Great Britain and Italy; there the economic costs of constant labor unrest take a heavy toll in falling productivity.

American labor unions have barely acknowledged worker-management cooperation as an option. Traditionally, American industrial unions have opposed worker-management joint schemes on the grounds that they would undermine the self-consciousness of labor. Exceptions, such as the Tarry-town, New York, General Motors plant, which has developed joint worker-management efforts to improve quality control and reduce absenteeism, have worked well.

American industrial labor, too, has as yet evidenced little inclination to bargain economic rights for long-term job security. In the steel industry, the rubber industry, and other major industries, 1980 negotiated wage increases hit the limit of the Council on Wage and Price Stability guidelines, 9.5 percent. But the United Auto Workers Union, with hundreds of thousands of members out of work, negotiated a 30-percent increase with the Chrysler Corporation over a three-year period.

Concentration of Economic Power

Finally, the new world economic order is characterized by the concentration of economic strength in large transnational and multinational corporations. These firms—whether conglomerates or specialized enterprises—are tightly controlled by a skilled management exercising control over billions in capital and millions of employees around the globe. In 1970 firms head-quartered in the United States but having majority-owned affiliates in other nations employed almost twelve million persons. In 1976 the Department of Commerce estimated their sales at $515 billion.

Among the consequences of multinational organization is the installa-tion of production facilities in lesser-developed countries to serve domestic markets, thereby reducing their reliance on American and European goods. Multinationals also finance large-scale production for international markets in low-cost nations, thus capturing available economies through cheap labor, proximity to natural resources, and tax and financial advantages. The economies of size and potential high returns attract investment capital and as a result limit the capital available to U.S. firms with limited, nation-al-market production capabilities. Confronting these challenges will be dif-ficult and cannot be achieved unilaterally. It is unrealistic to believe that multi-nationals will abandon their search for highest profits. Therefore government must take steps to increase the attractiveness of domestic pro-duction.

Concomitant with the growth of conglomerates and multinationals has been decreasing competitiveness of some small U.S. firms. Our corporate system encourages takeovers for financial reasons that are often unrelated to questions of output and productivity in the firms involved. The takeovers are rationalized with the idea that economies of size are advantageous. But size diseconomies have emerged which are not now recognized or acknow-ledged. Among them is the depressing effect of size on innovation. Several studies have shown—and many businessmen concur—that a majority of major innovations take place in minor organizations. Also, small firms are quicker to absorb new technologies than are giant enterprises. Thus, while maintenance of artificial competition through government regulation is absurd, small firms in some industries and sectors should be encouraged. Such efforts have been undertaken in Europe and Japan.

Challenge of the Eighties

It is no longer possible to ignore the challenges of this new international economic order. The conditions described—consolidation of economic power, increasing interdependencies among nations, increasing interaction between business and government in various forms of managed capitalism, increasing homogeneity and stability among economic groups within the advanced industrial countries, increasing pressures from poor countries for a larger share of world economic production—mean that the United States must develop new and improved approaches for managing its economy. Existing policies are too imprecise to meet the needs of such a complex economic system. Its enormous potential, fragmented nature, and frequent aberrations demand a comprehensive and integrated set of development-oriented policies. These policies must address opportunities for, and barriers to, increased output and increased efficiency in specific, economically significant industries.

Organization of the Book

The work is organized in five parts. Chapter 2 discusses causes for concern in the performance of the U.S. economy, particularly during the most recent period of cyclical change. Despite its continuing dominant position in the world economy, the United States is losing its premier spot according to several significant measures. Productivity rates are of particular concern. The relation of innovation and new capital investment to productivity is discussed. The issues are presented in a comparative context that suggests that if the present rates of change continue, the United States will continue to stagnate relative to other advanced industrial countries.

Chapter 3 describes recent and portended problems in selected sectors: a mature basic industry (steel); a young basic industry (aluminum); a high-technology light industry (semiconductors); a mature, consumer-goods sector (apparel); an emerging young sector (biochemicals); and the high-services sector. The impact of rates of innovation, technological change, actual and possible imports, and other market shifts in these and other critical economic activities must be analyzed before crises situations arise, so that a series of related steps—including fiscal, adjustment, and development measures—can be taken to strengthen the international competitive advantage of American firms.

The fourth chapter analyzes the major public interventions in the economy. While some of the consequences of fiscal, monetary, trade, regulatory, area, and limited sectoral policies now in effect are well understood and desired, other consequences are unintended and unwanted. The interrelationships among existing policies, and their significance for the future vitality of key sectors and industries, are explored. Foreign examples of integrated sectoral and regional policies are described.

Chapter 5 presents a set of measures necessary to national sectoral policies. The recommendations deal with policy goals and policy machinery, information requirements, and administrative reforms to enhance coordination and improve understanding of the outcomes of public intervention in the economy. Included are proposals for improved coordination within the federal government, improved coordination between the federal and subnational governments, and improved interaction between government and the private sector.

Note

1. John Shannon, "Overall Trends in Fiscal Federalism," Advisory Commission on Intergovernmental Relations, Draft, 1980. Chapter II, p. 1. The highest share, 35 percent, was occasioned in 1975; in 1977 it was 33 percent.

2 Causes for Concern

The economy of the United States is the largest and most diversified in the world. The $2.4 trillion gross national product (GNP) of the United States is almost equivalent to that of the nineteen European members of the Organization for Economic Cooperation and Development (OECD) and is almost three times larger than that of Japan.

But the U.S. economy is losing much of its vitality. Inflation threatens to be a permanent feature of the economy. Productivity has declined. American firms are no longer the world's major trend setters in terms of technological innovation. The level of productive capital investment has declined relative to GNP. The United States has the highest rate of unemployment of any major industrial power. American firms are losing competitiveness in both foreign and domestic markets.

These danger signs are matters for national concern even when considered in a historical context. To understand the danger signs, it is necessary to look at the absolute level of economic activity as well as recent and long-term trends. Comparing the trends of the giant U.S. economy with those of small industrial nations can create a misleading effect in that a given absolute gain in a small economy will create a larger percentage change than a similar gain in a larger economy. Even more important, mature sectors in a given economy cannot be expected to grow as rapidly as young or emerging sectors in the same or other economies.

Recent economic history can be dated from 1946. The United States was the only major industrial power to emerge from World War II with its domestic industrial base intact. This was a blessing that, ironically, was later to cause some problems. While Germany and Japan, Britain, France, and Italy, with U.S. help, rebuilt their basic industrial plants to modern standards of efficiency, U.S. firms continued to operate archaic production facilities, particularly in some of the most basic industries.

At the end of 1979 and the beginning of 1980, rampant inflation was certainly the number-one symptom of the nation's economic malaise. Consistently above the formerly intolerable level of 10 percent, inflation was driven by the high costs of basic resources—energy, food, and certain industrial raw materials—and of basic services, especially housing, transportation, and medical care. Inflation was not brought under control by high interest rates and tight money. Indeed, in many respects these policies

13

exacerbated the problem. To see the point, one only has to note that inflation in the housing sector was 15.2 percent at the beginning of 1980, despite nearly eight months of a monetary policy that skyrocketed mortgage prices and dried up mortgage funds in many large cities and suburbs.

Tight money in recent years seems to have fueled rather than curbed consumer spending. An inflationary psychology is now the norm. Expecting that their assets will continually be eroded by rising prices, consumers fall into the buy-now syndrome; there is little worry if they have no cash, for they can get credit. The phenomenal ballooning of consumer credit was finally recognized as an evil in the spring of 1980, but it had been going on for several years. Tight money, even with so-called voluntary wage constraints, did not exert a dampening effect on prices of most goods and services, in part because the wage floor, including cost-of-living increases, moved in lock-step with prices, and in part because plentiful credit kept those who had jobs buying.

Inflation can best be controlled by dealing with supply-side costs as well as with demand. First, of course, it is absolutely essential to find substitutes for imported oil so that OPEC does not set the nation's inflation rate. Until we do so, we must curb consumption of energy at least enough to offset the impact of rising prices. Second, we must get more out of every dollar invested in human labor and in capital equipment. We must increase the productivity of workers, both through improving their performance and through seeing to it that every industry is using the most modern and efficient equipment possible.

Living Standards and Productivity

Initially as a result of the need for reconstruction, but later for other reasons as well, the post-World War II annual growth rates in gross domestic products (GDP)[1] of Germany, Japan, France, and Italy have been consistently higher than that of the United States (see table 2–1). Canada, a less-diversified and less-mature economy that also escaped war damage, also grew faster economically than did the United States. Cumulatively, these differential growth rates have created substantial shifts in the relative economic strengths of the United States and other major industrial nations. In 1950, the per capita GDP of Japan was 18 percent of that of the United States. By 1977 this had increased to 63 percent (see table 2–2). Canada increased its relative per capita GDP from 80 percent of that of the United States in 1950 to 98 percent in 1977.

Does this really matter? Yes. The point about relative per capita gross domestic product is not its absolute magnitude but the processes it reflects. Faster GDP growth reflects expanding output as well as increasing produc-

Table 2–1

Average Annual Growth in Per Capita Gross Domestic Product, 1950–1977

Time Period	United States	Canada	France	Germany	Italy	United Kingdom	Japan
1950–1960	3.2	4.6	4.8	8.5	5.5	2.8	8.0
1960–1970	3.9	5.2	5.6	4.7	5.5	2.8	11.1
1970–1977	3.1	4.8	4.0	2.6	2.8	1.9	5.2
1950–1977	3.4	4.9	4.9	5.5	4.8	2.6	8.5

Source: *Statistical Abstract of the United States: 1979* (100th edition) (Washington, D.C.: U.S. Bureau of the Census, 1979).

Table 2–2

Gross Domestic Product of Selected Countries

Country	Per Capita GDP as Percentage of U.S. GDP						
	1950	1960	1965	1970	1975	1976	1977
Canada	80	84	86	91	101	101	98
France	54	69	73	82	90	89	88
West Germany	50	84	87	94	95	96	95
Italy	25	35	37	44	44	44	43
Japan	18	28	37	57	63	63	63
United Kingdom	53	58	56	56	57	56	55

Source: *Statistical Abstract of the United States: 1979* (100th edition) (Washington, D.C.: Bureau of the Census, 1979).

tivity growth rates. Fast-growing nations are building the capacity for future growth and investment.

Jobs and Economic Growth

Before turning to a discussion of productivity, however, let us first look at how the United States has fared in terms of providing jobs for its citizens. Among the major industrial nations of the world, the United States has both the largest civilian labor force and the highest national level of unemployment (see table 2–3).

The United States, unlike other advanced industrial countries, saw a very large increase in its labor force during the decade of the 1970s; almost

18 million persons joined the labor force during the period 1970–1978, which represented a 21-percent increase. The coming of age of many children born in the 1950s and 1960s and the increased participation of women in the work force placed new pressures on the economy to generate jobs. Illegal immigrants and refugees swelled the work force in parts of the country during the late 1970s. The demographic pressures will not taper off until 1985; the number and proportion of women in the labor force will likely increase.

Other nations have not had to grapple with a rapidly swelling work force. West Germany, which had a labor shortage and depended on imported labor during the boom period of the 1960s, was able to shrink its civilian work force by almost 1 million persons during the slow-growth 1976–1978 period by sending workers back to their native countries. Japan has been able to keep its unemployment levels between rates of 1.2 percent and 2.3 percent, in part by shifting workers from industry to industry or from productive to nonproductive activities, such as beautifying the factory grounds. Other nations have done almost as well. West Germany, France, and Italy have been able to operate within quasi-market economies, to improve productivity and overall levels of production, and to maintain lower unemployment levels than that of the United States.

Productivity and Economic Growth

Growth in the nation's productivity—the relationship between the quantity of goods and services produced and the quantity of labor and capital

Table 2-3
Labor Force and Unemployment: International Comparisons, 1970–1978

Country	Civilian Labor Force (millions)			Percentage Unemployed		
	1970	1974	1978	1970	1974	1978
United States	82.7	91.0	100.4	4.9	5.6	6.0
Canada	8.4	9.7	10.9	5.7	5.4	8.4
France	21.0	21.7	22.2	2.6	3.0	5.4
West Germany	26.3	26.1	25.3	.8	1.7	3.4
Italy	20.0	20.1	20.6	3.1	2.8	3.5
United Kingdom	24.3	24.5	25.4	3.1	2.9	6.1
Japan	50.7	52.4	54.6	1.2	1.4	2.3

Source: *Statistical Abstract of the United States: 1979* (100th edition) (Washington, D.C.: U.S. Bureau of the Census, 1979).

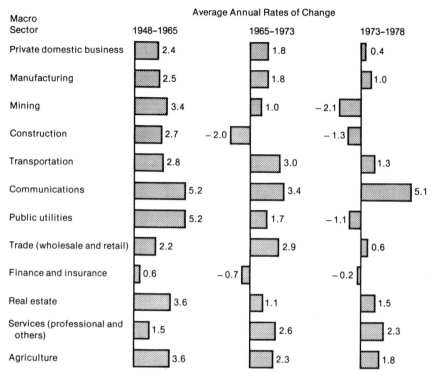

Source: Carolyn Meanly, ed., *Productivity Perspectives* (Houston: American Productivity Center, 1980).

Figure 2-1. Changes in Productivity, 1948-1978

required to produce them—has declined relative to both past performance and the productivity growth of other nations. It is often asserted that one cause of slower overall productivity increases is the relatively high proportion of employment in the service sectors, which are more labor-intensive than the manufacturing sectors. But in the manufacturing sectors, the trend in the 1970s was very slow growth in productivity, while the rate of change in the service sectors sensitive to computerization was relatively high (see figure 2-1). Productivity change measured by output per employee per hour in the manufacturing macro sector fell from an annual average increase of 2.7 percent in the period 1950-1967 to an annual average increase of 2.1 percent in the period of 1967-1975 (see table 2-4). The worst news is that any productivity growth is no longer to be taken for granted. In 1979 the actual level of labor productivity fell.

In manufacturing activities, the U.S. productivity growth rate has been smaller than the growth rates of Japan, Germany, France, Canada, and the

Table 2–4

Average Annual Percentage Change in Output per Employee-Hour in Manufacturing, 1950–1975

Country	1950–1975	1950–1967	1967–1975
United States	2.6	2.7	2.1
Japan	9.2	8.6	8.2
Germany	6.0	6.2	5.2
Canada	4.1	4.1	3.6
France	5.3	4.9	4.6
United Kingdom	3.4	3.0	3.2

Source: Bureau of Labor Statistics, *Productivity and the Economy,* Bulletin 1926 (Washington, D.C.: U.S. Department of Labor, 1977).

Table 2–5

Long-Term International Productivity Dynamics: Levels and Trends of Real Gross Domestic Products per Employee-Hour, 1950–1977

Nation	Gross Domestic Product Per Hour [a]		Average Annual Growth Rate	
	1950	1977	1950–1970	1970–1977
(Arithmetic Average)	46	74	4.4	3.8
Australia	70	78	2.6	3.0
Austria	29	66	5.9	4.7
Belgium	53	94	4.0	5.8
Canada	78	88	2.9	2.2
Denmark	44	66	4.1	3.2
Finland	32	66	5.4	4.3
France	41	79	4.8	5.1
Germany	35	84	6.2	4.7
Italy	31	68	5.4	5.0
Japan	14	52	7.9	5.7
Netherlands	51	84	4.1	4.6
Norway	49	86	4.7	3.8
Sweden	57	79	4.1	2.0
Switzerland	51	65	3.5	2.8
United Kingdom	55	61	2.8	2.4
United States	100	100	2.5	2.0

Source: Carolyn Meanley, ed., *Productivity Perspectives,* (Houston: American Productivity Center, 1980).

[a]GDP is measured in constant 1970 U.S. price and exchange rates.

United Kingdom (see table 2-5). All these advanced industrial nations seemed to have slowed their productivity gains; during the last decade their productivity gains, including that of the United States, fell relative to the period 1950-1970. However, the decline in the rate was steepest in the United States. This reflects declining real capital-investment levels and, to a very limited degree, may reflect absorption of new labor-force entrants who are generally less productive than experienced workers. Without productivity increases, little if any improvement in the real standard of living can take place.

The major concern for the future, therefore, is the competitive edge. Although in aggregate terms the United States is still one of the most productive economies in the world, other nations are rapidly narrowing the productivity differential. In 1978 West Germany produced 85 percent as much per worker overall as the United States did, and Japan little more than half as much. But for selected macro sectors, the productivity gap has been closed, and U.S. firms are not competitive—manufacturing, mining, and construction being the most sluggish macro sectors.

There are two ways in which productivity can be increased. One is by improving the quality of work force performance. The other is through mechanization or automation that substitutes machine work for human work, or increases the pace at which machine work is performed, or improves the quality of machine work.

Capital Investment

Several recent studies have attempted to isolate and quantify the various factors contributing to productivity growth. In 1977 a Department of Labor report, *Productivity and the Economy,* compared three independent evaluations of the contribution of capital, labor, and technology to the productivity of the U.S. economy in the post World War II period (see table 2-6). Although there are some differences in the definitions, concepts, and assumptions underlying these three studies, they offer a range of estimates of the relative contributions of the three factors to past productivity increases. Labor's performance contributes from 10 to 18 percent; new technology from 44 to 62 percent; and capital plant and equipment from 18 to 42 percent.

The rate at which new, efficient machinery and facilities are introduced into any industry is measured by comparing investment in equipment and plant to the value of all goods and services produced. This ratio was apparently higher during the 1970s than in previous decades, reaching nearly 10 percent on average for the period 1970-1978 (see table 2-7).

On a closer look, however, it appears that a substantial portion of total

Table 2–6
Factors Contributing to Industrial Productivity
(percentage)

Factors	Denison[a]	Kendrick[a]	Christensen/ Cummings/ Jorgenson[a]
Capital	20	18	42
Labor quality	18	10	14
Technology[b]	62	72	44

Source: Bureau of Labor Statistics, *Productivity and the Economy,* (Washington, D.C.: U.S. Department of Labor, 1977).

[a] The studies compared by this report are Edward F. Denison, *Accounting for United States Economic Growth, 1929–1969.* John W. Kendrick, *Postwar Productivity Trends in the United States, 1948–69.* Laurits R. Christensen, Dianne Cummings, and Dale W. Jorgensen, *An International Comparison of Growth in Productivity, 1947–1973.*

[b] Technology refers to all factors other than labor quality and capital. It is residual. Differences in the measuring the labor and capital factors create different residuals.

nonresidential fixed capital investment does not find its way into the production process. For example, certain environmental-protection and worker-safety and health regulations are forcing some industries and sectors to divert capital to nonproductive facilities. In 1979 it was estimated that 18 percent of steel-industry investment went for pollution-control equipment.[2] This means, in effect, that the real rate of production-related capital expenditure as a proportion of GNP is declining. The diversion rate varies by sector, by industry, and by locality. Naturally, investment in pollution control and worker safety is important. But it is important to recognize the effects of diversion, because a strongly declining rate of real productive investment will in the long run have a negative influence on the overall growth of productivity and on the competitive advantage of American firms making this investment as compared to foreign firms and overseas subsidiaries of U.S. firms that are not required to divert capital to this function.

The downward trend is corroborated by other indicators. The efficiency of capital utilization is one measure of productivity in the industrial sectors. The ratio of the value of output to the value of capital stock measures efficiency. If the value of output increases faster than the real value of the stock (even though additions to the stock are being made), then the economy is becoming more efficient. If, on the other hand, the value of the stock is rising faster than the rate of increase in output, the economy is in trouble, at least temporarily, because productivity is either stagnant or declining. These trends must be observed over a few years, since productivity increases generated by new plant and equipment will show up not in

Table 2–7
Nonresidential Fixed Investment as a Percentage of Gross National Product

Year	Current Dollars	Constant 1972 Dollars
1950	9.5	9.4
1951	9.4	9.2
1952	9.0	8.7
1953	9.4	9.1
1954	9.3	9.0
1955	9.6	9.3
1956	10.4	9.7
1957	10.5	9.7
1958	9.3	8.7
1959	9.3	8.7
1960	9.4	9.0
1961	9.0	8.7
1962	9.1	8.9
1963	9.0	8.8
1964	9.4	9.3
1965	10.4	10.3
1966	10.8	10.8
1967	10.3	10.3
1968	10.3	10.3
1969	10.6	10.6
1970	10.2	10.2
1971	9.8	9.8
1972	10.0	10.0
1973	10.4	10.6
1974	10.7	10.7
1975	9.8	9.4
1976	9.7	9.3
1977	10.0	9.6
1978	10.4	10.0

Source: Calculated by Bureau of Economic Analysis, U.S. Department of Commerce, Washington, D.C., 1979.

the year the investment is made but a year or two later, when the labor force has adapted to the new facilities and functions at its highest performance level. Thus, over a decade, an increase in the ratio between rate of change in output and rate of change in stock signals rising efficiency.

During the 1970s, this ratio increased slightly over the 1960s average, from .601 for the ten-year average of the 1960s to .616 for the nine-year average of the 1970s (see table 2–8). Since the 1974 recession, this productivity measure has remained at a level substantially below that of the economic boom period of the late 1960s. Although it is probably unjustifiable to hope for boomtime productivity levels, and although the long-term ratio is definitely upward, it is reasonable to expect that the low rate of increase in value of stock experienced during the period after 1975 will reduce the efficiency ratio during the early 1980s.

A third indicator of possible capital-investment shortages, and future problems with productivity as a result, is the maturation of the existing capital stock. If existing buildings are not replaced or modernized and old equipment is not replaced by more efficient equipment, the opportunity for increased productivity will be reduced. This lack of investment will be measured by increasing average age of the stock. Again, equipment is the key factor, and the average age of manufacturing equipment in the United States is now 6.4 years.[3] While this equipment is "younger" than it was ten years ago, it is not *growing younger* as fast as it was in the 1960s. The question that cannot be definitely answered is whether this decline is a problem or merely a phenomenon. It may be that the equipment in use is new and modern enough; or it may be that the flattening of the rate of new investment, particularly in relation to the large numbers of unemployed that the economy cannot absorb, will further depress productivity.

It has been popular to call for across-the-board incentives to investment as the panacea for low productivity and stagflation. But the evidence suggests that a more carefully tailored set of investment incentives would be more successful and less wasteful. Only those sectors and industries vital to the economy, for which new capital investment is needed (and lacking) to meet explicit production and output goals, should be subsidized by government and taxpayers. The most efficient approach would seem to be to evaluate capital investment in given sectors and industries, in competing countries, in the context of their rates of growth and productivity relative to the United States, and then to determine whether, for a given industry or sector, a domestic problem of capital formation exists.

Technological Innovation

Technological innovation is a major contributor to increases in productivity. Economists have estimated that new technology contributed from 44 percent to 72 percent to productivity increases (see table 2–6).

Innovation itself is a concept that embraces several elements. In order to determine whether the country is lagging in innovation, most economists

Table 2-8
Nonfinancial Corporations, Output and Stocks, 1950–1978
(1972 dollars)

Year	Output	Stocks at Mid Year	Stocks at Year End	Output/ Stock
1950	247.5	493.4	500.7	.502
1951	270.2	509.8	518.8	.530
1952	275.2	527.6	536.4	.522
1953	292.0	546.3	556.1	.535
1954	283.5	564.8	573.4	.502
1955	315.1	583.6	593.8	.540
1956	324.1	605.1	616.4	.536
1957	328.3	627.6	638.8	.523
1958	313.4	645.9	652.9	.485
1959	347.3	660.7	668.4	.526
1960	358.9	677.5	686.5	.530
1961	366.7	694.8	703.0	.528
1962	398.7	713.0	723.0	.561
1963	425.4	732.9	742.8	.580
1964	455.2	754.9	766.9	.603
1965	494.6	783.9	800.9	.631
1966	532.9	821.2	841.5	.649
1967	545.8	860.4	879.2	.634
1968	581.6	899.0	918.8	.646
1969	607.3	940.5	962.1	.646
1970	600.6	981.1	1,000.0	.612
1971	619.3	1,017.4	1,034.8	.609
1972	671.0	1,054.4	1,073.9	.636
1973	720.4	1,097.9	1,121.8	.657
1974	695.0	1,145.3	1,168.7	.607
1975	680.0	1,184.0	1,199.3	.574
1976	730.4	1,214.9	1,230.4	.601
1977	770.7	1,251.0	1,271.6	.617
1978	818.7	1,293.8	1,315.9	.633

Source: Bureau of Economic Analysis, U.S. Department of Commerce, Unpublished, 1979.

measure the total amount of new or improved products, processes, and services. But the type of innovation is equally important. It is particularly significant to distinguish between producer-goods and consumer-goods innovations. A new form of throwaway product, such as paper clothes or a cereal that sings rather than popping, will not contribute as much to total productivity as a new microchip or a laser beam. Furthermore, in addition to merely counting patents, we must consider the rate at which innovations are absorbed into the economy. The existence of a vast number of new products or processes is of little value if they are not being utilized or if the cost of utilizing them outweighs the benefits (profits) anticipated from their introduction.

The recent performance of American firms in the area of innovation gives genuine cause for alarm. Both relative to past performance and relative to the recent and current performance of other nations, the rate of technological advance in the United States is unfavorable. There has been an absolute decline in research and development efforts as a percentage of GNP. The number of patents issued to domestic recipients is lower relative to the number issued to foreign individuals and firms. The very nature of innovation is shifting. The technological capacity of other nations is growing, partly as a result of American firms' increasingly prevalent practice of exporting the newest, most advanced technology to other countries for final development and use.

Research and Development

Research and development (R&D) is the engine of technological advance. In the United States both the public and the private sectors finance R&D. In 1979 government spent approximately $25.7 billion on R&D and private

Table 2-9
Research and Development Expenditures, 1960–1979
(billions of dollars)

Performance Sector	1960	1965	1970	1973	1975	1977	1979[a]
Total research and development	13.5	20.0	25.9	30.6	35.2	42.9	51.6
Percentage federal as a source	64.6	64.9	56.6	53.3	51.6	50.5	49.8
Total basic and applied research	4.2	6.8	9.2	10.5	12.4	15.3	18.4
Percentage federal as a source	31.1	40.6	40.9	39.8	39.3	38.7	NA
Total basic research	1.2	2.5	3.5	3.8	4.5	5.4	6.7
Percentage federal as a source	13.4	14.2	15.4	13.9	15.1	15.9	NA
Total research and development as a percentage of gross national product	2.6	2.9	2.6	2.3	2.3	2.2	2.4

Source: *Statistical Abstract of the United States: 1979* (100th edition) (Washington, D.C.: U.S. Bureau of the Census, 1979).
[a] Estimated values.

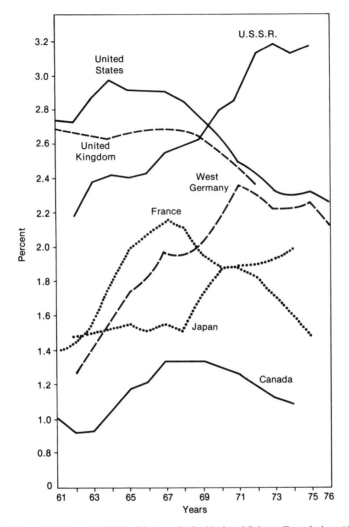

Source: *Science Indicators, 1976* (Washington, D.C.: National Science Foundation, 1977).
Figure 2-2. National Expenditures for Performance of R&D as a
Percentage of Gross National Product, by Country, 1961–1976

corporations spent $25.9 billion (see table 2-9). During each of the last 15
years, however, private R&D as a proportion of GNP has fallen. In the
booming mid-1960s, R&D in aggregate constituted almost 3 percent of
GNP, but by 1979 it represented little more than 2.4 percent—a substantial
relative drop. Although some other countries, notably the United Kingdom,
Canada, and West Germany, experienced similar declines, the drop has

been less precipitous (see figure 2–2). Japan tries harder, and continues to spend more on R&D both absolutely and relatively. Thus, although in aggregate the United States spends more on R&D absolutely than any other western country and still enjoys an overall technological superiority because of past activities, the failure to keep up the pace of research and development could mean that in the future more individual industries will be challenged by foreign firms on the basis of technological parity or even superiority.

Another aspect of the R&D problem is the type of investigation being supported. As shown in table 2–10, the United States devotes a substantially greater portion of its research funds to military and space functions than do other industrialized Western nations. Japan and West Germany, which since World War II have been largely dependent on the United States for military defense, are devoting large amounts of government research funds to civilian technological research in agriculture, forestry, fisheries, mining, manufacturing, transportation, telecommunications, construction, and urban and rural planning and development. While it is certainly true that defense- and space-related R&D in the United States produced many bene-

Table 2–10
Estimated Distribution of Government R&D Expenditures among Selected Areas, by Country, 1961–1973

National Objectives	Percentage Distribution			
Canada	1961–1962	1966–1967	1970–1971	1974–1975
National defense	24	17	9	8
Space	NA	2	1	4
Energy production	18	21	18	14
Economic development	46	43	50	43
Health	4	7	10	9
Community services	a	2	2	12
Advancement of knowledge[b]	8	8	8	10
France	1961	1967	1972	1975
National defense	44	35	28	30
Space	1	6	7	6
Energy production	25	20	15	9
Economic development	8	16	20	26
Health	a	1	2	4
Community services	a	1	2	2
Advancement of knowledge	20	20	26	24

Table 2-10 continued

National Objectives	Percentage Distribution			
Japan	*1961–1962*	*1965–1966*	*1969–1970*	*1974–1975*
National defense	4	3	2	2
Space	—	a	1	5
Energy production	7	3	8	8
Economic development	30	27	23	23
Health	1	2	2	3
Community services	1	2	2	3
Advancement of knowledge	56	63	61	55
United Kingdom	*1961–1962*	*1966–1967*	*1972–1973*	*1974–1975*
National defense	65	52	43	47
Space	1	4	2	2
Energy production	15	13	9	6
Economic development	10	14	23	21
Health	2	3	5	2
Community services	a	a	1	1
Advancement of knowledge	7	12	15	20
United States	*1961–1962*	*1966–1967*	*1971–1972*	*1974–1975*
National defense	71	49	53	51
Space	12	32	18	13
Energy production	7	5	5	6
Economic development	3	5	8	9
Health	5	6	9	12
Community services	1	2	5	5
Advancement of knowledge[b]	1	2	3	4
West Germany	*1961*	*1966*	*1971*	*1975*
National defense	22	19	15	11
Space	—	4	6	4
Energy production	16	16	16	11
Economic development	NA	NA	13	14
Health	NA	NA	3	3
Community services	NA	NA	2	6
Advancement of knowledge	37	35	41	51

Source: Organization for Economic Cooperation and Development, *Changing Priorities for Government R&D* (Paris: OECD, 1975), and OECD, *International Statistical Year, 1973: The Objectives of Government R&D Funding, 1970–76,* Vol. 2B (Paris: OECD, 1977).

Note: Percentage may not total 100 because of exclusion of the category "Not specified" and/or due to rounding.

[a] Less than 0.5 percent.

[b] Excludes general university funds.

ficial spin-offs for civilian commercial applications, the United States must not become complacent in assuming such positive outcomes. In selected sectors it may well be in the national interest to earmark government funds for specific lines of inquiry or, as will be discussed further, for building prototype systems and subsidizing initial production runs.

The potential technological competitiveness of foreign producers appears to be growing more rapidly than that of the United States by virtue of the greater number of patents issued to foreign individuals and firms. The number of U.S. patents granted to U.S. inventors has declined steadily since 1971. The number of U.S. patents granted to foreign inventors and firms has increased almost every year since 1963. Consequently, the share of patents granted to foreigners as a percentage of total patents issued has increased to the point that in 1979 they represented 38 percent of all patents issued by the United States—more than a doubling of foreign inventor activities in the United States in the period 1961-1978 (see table 2-11). The National Science Foundation (NSF) reported that in the period 1963-1975 the share of U.S. patents held by foreign investors increased in nearly every product field. Between 1970 and 1975, the patenting of Japanese firms increased by 100 percent in almost every industrial field. West German firms and individuals also secured substantially more patents. Thus foreign firms have strengthened their technological abilities in comparison with U.S. industries through control of the key ingredient, proprietary technology.

During the early 1970s, when foreign firms were acquiring or creating proprietary technology, the very nature of American technological research appeared to be changing. Radical breakthroughs accounted for almost 36 percent of all innovations in the period 1953-1959 but only 16 percent in the period 1967-1973, according to the NSF (see table 2-12). Instead of miracle inventions, such as the laser beam, the microchip, and the xerographic process, research seemed until very recently to be producing mutations and adaptations of known ideas. We wish to avoid overdramatizing this point, especially because in the field of biochemistry the end of the 1970s witnessed some revolutionary discoveries, notably the ability to create living matter. However, it is true that one outcome of such breakthroughs as laser and microwave technology was to greatly increase industrial productivity, whereas the radical breakthroughs of the present generation tend more to open up new areas for industrial and commercial development. Both thrusts are needed to lay the foundation for future economic activity as well as to solve health and environmental-safety problems.

One reason that there may be relatively fewer innovative breakthroughs now than there were twenty years ago is that the creative atmosphere and uninhibited environment needed to nurture what someone once called the "Aha" approach to research is less prevalent now than it used to be. The

Table 2-11
Issuance of U.S. Patents to Domestic and Foreign Corporations, 1961-1978
(thousands)

	1961-1965	*1966-1970*	*1973*	*1976*	*1978*
United States corporations	152.5	190.6	38.6	34.3	31.3
Foreign corporations	30.9	52.7	16.5	19.9	19.2
Total	183.4	243.3	55.1	54.2	50.5
Patents issued to foreign corporations as a percentage of the total	16.8	21.6	29.9	36.7	38.0

Source: *Statistical Abstract of the United States: 1979* (100th edition) (Washington, D.C.: U.S. Bureau of the Census, 1979).

Table 2-12
Major U.S. Innovations, 1953-1973

Classification	*1953-1973*	*1953-1959*	*1960-1966*	*1967-1973*
	Percentage Distribution			
Total	100	100	100	100
Major breakthrough	26	36	26	16
Major technological shift	28	17	31	35
Improvement	38	39	37	40
Imitation or no new technology	8	8	6	10
	Number of Innovations			
Total	250	75	94	81
Major breakthrough	64	27	24	13
Major technological shift	70	13	29	28
Improvement	96	29	35	32
Imitation or no new technology	20	6	6	8

Source: *Science Indicators, 1976* (Washington, D.C.: National Science Foundation, 1977).

reason is that fewer small firms can afford to foster basic research, while large firms tend to control either the research or its development, or both, thus dampening enthusiasm for invention outside of university laboratories. Small firms traditionally were the wellsprings of experimentation leading to technological innovation in this country. NSF reports that firms of fewer than 1,000 employees produce substantially more technological innovations per research dollar than large firms of 10,000 and more employees (see table 2-13). Yet during the period 1969-1979, the rate of formation of new, small firms seems to have fallen, while absorption of small firms has been on the rise. Thus, one of the primary sources of innovation—the small firm—is rapidly losing its position as a force in national economic and industrial activity.

In many cases existing small firms cannot get access to the capital they need to try new ventures or to manufacture new products in sufficiently large runs to be profitable, even though it is often the case that small firms can enter new production more rapidly and even more efficiently than large ones.

Operations and Innovation

Innovation itself is of little practical significance unless it is put to use in a way to increase profits and/or productivity. It is alarming that much of the new technology created in the United States is not being put to use in the United States but is increasingly being sold or licensed to foreign firms. The royalties and fees gained by U.S. firms for production rights to foreign firms increased over 250 percent in the period 1970-1978 from $2.1 billion in 1970 to almost $5.3 billion in 1978.[4] Much of the rapid growth in these sales has occurred particularly since 1972.

While the products produced by overseas licensees might eventually find themselves back in American markets, perhaps at prices lower than those possible if the goods were produced under current practices in the United States, their production overseas deprives the United States of jobs, taxes, and economic multipliers.

Much of the technology being sold is not just mature technology but the most advanced. These technology transfers built the foundation for much of the industrial expansion made by Japan and other nations in the 1960s and 1970s. It now appears, however, that the Japanese themselves are becoming major generators of basic technology. While continuing to buy specific technologies from the United States and third parties, the Japanese have greatly increased government and private investments in basic R&D.

One reason that American firms having control over new technology may be exporting it is the many domestic barriers to absorption. Firms may have trouble financing new-product development. They may find after-tax profits too unappealing, especially compared to free-zone opportunities abroad. Government regulations regarding product standards, workplace, and environmental impact discourage production here because they create high uncertainty costs, or because firms simply want to avoid them. While

Table 2–13

Distribution of Major U.S. Innovations by Size of Company, 1953–1973

Period	Total	Size of Company				
		Up to 100 Employees	100–1,000 Employees	1,000–5,000 Employees	5,000–10,000 Employees	10,000 or More Employees
		Percentage Distribution				
1953–1973	100	23	24	13	5	34
1953–1959	100	23	26	14	8	29
1960–1966	100	27	23	14	5	31
1967–1973	100	20	23	12	3	43
		Number of Innovations				
1953–1973	310	72	75	41	16	106
1953–1959	102	23	27	14	8	30
1960–1966	197	29	25	15	5	33
1967–1973	101	20	23	12	3	43

Source: *Science Indicators, 1976* (Washington, D.C.: National Science Foundation, 1977).

we do not favor turning back the clock of social progress, it is imperative that social goals be pursued with maximum clarity and consistency if domestic development is to compete favorably with overseas options.

Testimony before the Senate Committee on Science and Technology and the Joint Economic Committee indicates that only very large firms have sufficient financial and technical capacity to cope with the costs associated with putting new technologies into the operational phase. Other evidence suggests, however, that small firms accomplish this more readily. For example, American Motors, the smallest U.S. auto company, retooled to produce energy-efficient cars faster than GM, Ford, or Chrysler. There may be untapped opportunities for smaller firms in other sectors to adapt new technologies if they are given access to financing.

Summary: Technological Drag

By the measures of relative R&D expenditures, patent balances, and export of technology, the U.S. position as the world's dominant scientific and engineering nation is threatened. Encouraging technological innovation, especially for domestic production, is a necessary and legitimate public-policy concern. There is a strong need for close examination of the nature, pace, and barriers to technological advance. Evaluation of the incentives to and reasons for export of critical technology is particularly needed. While new programs to encourage research and development may also be necessary, such efforts would be entirely wasted if, as their result, the supply of exportable technology was increased but the domestic absorption rate was not.

International Balance of Trade

One barrier to domestic production is undoubtedly foreign protectionism. Both developed and developing nations have erected numerous nontariff barriers to protect their domestic infant industries and to encourage foreign-owned production facilities on their soil.

It is a truism familiar to most Americans that the Japanese have evidenced an extraordinary capacity to take select American-developed innovations, such as transistors and television, create high-quality products, and market them in the United States at prices so competitive with those of American products that they have come to dominate the market. Now, in fact, most television-set components are produced overseas, and production by U.S. firms in the United States is virtually defunct. A similar process has occurred in consumer electronics, such as calculators. The miniaturization of storage capacity, the major breakthrough in computer technology during the 1970s, was engineered in the United States, but both U.S. firms with overseas operations and foreign firms are competing strongly for sales of miniature components and systems.

If imports provide consumers with better products at lower prices, is there a cause for concern? Yes. A country that imports more than it exports has a deficit in the balance of trade. If the value of its total goods/services imports, including returns to capital, exceeds the value of its total goods/services exports, it also has a deficit in the balance of payments. Persistent deficits undermine the value of the country's currency on the international money exchange.

Large, persistent deficits in the U.S. balance of payments during the 1970s undermined the value of the dollar as the primary medium of international exchange. Although the deflation of the dollar was generally assumed to promise a long-term beneficial impact on the balance of trade—because U.S. firms can export more goods priced in dollars when the dollar falls relative to other currencies, and consumers tend to import less because imports become more expensive—dollar devaluation increases the domestic inflation rate. There is no unanimous agreement on the relationship between devaluation and inflation rates, but Charles Schultze estimates that the direct and indirect effect of a 10-percent devaluation is a 1.5-percent increase in inflation.[5]

The relative values of imports and exports constantly fluctuate due to international monetary shifts and domestic price changes, and therefore the significance of trends in relative value is not always clear. Unit value is a measure of trade flows, taking into account price and quantity (see table 2–14). By the unit-value measure, the U.S. trade deficit rose continuously throughout the 1970s. The 1979 trade deficit totaled approximately $43 billion.[6] Much of this, of course, was incurred as a result of the continued high volume of imported oil, which, though lower than the peak import year of 1977, still exceeded the $39 billion level. However, an increasing share of the deficit was attributable to manufactured goods rather than raw materials, a particular cause for concern. The United States imported over $100 billion of manufactured goods in 1978, an increase of 400 percent over 1970 (see table 2–15). By contrast, the U.S. share of world exports of manufactures has fallen steadily for many years (see table 2–16). The U.S. export position in world trade is decidedly less favorable than that of its major competitors in the OECD.

Table 2–14
Index of the Unit Values of Imports and Exports—Selected Nations 1970–1978

Country	1970	1974	1976	1978
United States				
Export	57	89	104	119
Import	46	93	103	121
Japan				
Export	55	100	99	134
Import	40	95	103	116
France				
Export	49	84	98	120
Import	48	91	99	118
Germany				
Export	51	89	100	126
Import	52	95	101	123
Italy				
Export	51	88	94	117
Import	41	95	98	117
United Kingdom				
Export	57	86	98	134
Import	57	93	99	126
Canada				
Export	56	94	106	106
Import	61	90	104	112

Source: *Statistical Abstract of the United States: 1979* (100th edition) (Washington, D.C.: U.S. Bureau of the Census, 1979).
Note: Indexes in U.S. dollars, 1975 = 100. A unit value is an implicit price derived from value and quantity data.

Table 2-15
U.S. Merchandise Exports and Imports by Commodity Groups, 1958–1979
(millions of dollars)

Year	Merchandise Exports					Merchandise Imports			
	Total Domestic and Foreign Exports	Domestic Exports				General Imports			
		Total	Food Beverages, and Tobacco	Crude Materials and Fuels	Manufactured Goods	Total	Food, Beverages, and Tobacco	Crude Materials and Fuels	Manufactured Goods
		F.a.s. Value				*Customs Value*			
1960	19,659	19,459	3,167	3,942	12,583	15,073	3,392	4,418	6,863
1965	26,742	26,399	4,519	4,273	17,433	21,427	4,013	5,440	11,244
1970	42,659	42,025	5,058	6,692	29,344	39,951	6,230	6,542	25,907
1975	107,589	106,100	16,793	15,197	70,951	96,570	9,923	32,596	51,080
1976	115,150	113,476	17,234	16,095	77,241	121,009	11,891	41,474	64,775
1977	121,150	118,944	15,963	18,579	80,151	147,685	14,227	53,554	76,554
1978	143,575	141,069	20,626	20,952	94,484	172,026	15,742	51,913	100,352

Source: *Economic Report of the President*, Washington, D.C., 1980.

Table 2-16
U.S. Share of World Exports of Manufactures. 1960-1977
(percentage)

Item	1960	1965	1970	1971	1972	1973	1974	1975	1976	1977
Total manufactures	25	23	21	19	18	18	19	19	19	17
Nonelectric machinery	33	31	28	26	25	25	26	28	27	25
Transport equipment	33	28	29	30	26	27	29	28	25	24
Chemicals	30	25	22	20	19	19	19	20	21	21
Electric machinery	28	24	23	21	21	22	23	22	23	23

Source: *Statistical Abstract of the United States: 1979*, (Washington, D.C.: U.S. Department of Commerce, 1979).

Import Penetration and Worldwide Competition

Many of the OECD exports are destined for the United States. Such consumer durables as cars, television sets, and cameras are not the only types of product in demand, however. Producer durables, including scientific instruments, complex electronic equipment for monitoring large systems such as electric power stations, and the component parts for building such systems, make up an increasingly large proportion of United States imports from Germany, France, Japan, Switzerland, and other advanced nations. This "import penetration" in the most advanced equipment should be a cause for major concern in the United States.

A simple way to measure import penetration of the domestic economy is to examine the ratio between imports and gross national product. If the ratio is increasing, imports are capturing more of domestic markets. Of course, the aggregate figures alone tell nothing about the causes of rising import penetration, and the causes are not necessarily bad news. For example, in a given industrial sector, imports may consist of low-priced goods that domestic producers ignore in preference for high-end products. Or, in a given sector, increasing imports may reflect temporary saturation of domestic production capacity. Thus the fact that in a given industry imports are rising faster than output of domestic products is not in and of itself a cause for countervailing action. It is, however, a signal that investigation is in order. It may mean that overseas producers are being subsidized to flood U.S. and other markets with low-priced goods. It may mean that supply bottlenecks are crippling American producers. It may mean that there is an urgent need for new capital to modernize U.S. plants, or it may signal a number of other problems that government policy should address.

Between 1970 and 1978, imports as a proportion of GNP increased from 6 percent to 10 percent (see table 2–17). The big jump followed the 1973 oil embargo, but OPEC alone is not responsible for America's growing dependency on imports.

Source of Imports

Japan is our major competitor in production of manufactured goods. Imports from Japan to the United States have been consistently greater during the last decade than imports from any other country, totaling $25.8 billion in 1978. Japan's exports to the United States have increased markedly in the last seven years, even though the rates of increase of imports from countries other than Japan have exceeded the rate of increase in Japanese imports in very recent years. Imports from Japan increased 166 percent during that period. Japanese imports in 1979 amount to 12.7

Table 2-17
Imports and Exports as a Percentage of Gross National Product, 1960–1978
(billions of dollars)

Item	1960	1965	1970	1971	1972	1973	1974	1975	1976	1977	1978
Gross National Product	506	688	982	1,063	1,171	1,307	1,412	1,528	1,700	1,887	2,108
Exports of goods and services	28	40	63	65.6	73	102	138	147	163	176	205
Imports of goods and services	23	32	59	64.0	76	94	132	127	156	187	217
Net exports of goods and services	5	8	4	1.6	-3	8	6	20	7	-11	-12
Total value of exports plus imports	51	72	122	129.6	149	196	270	274	319	362	422
Imports plus exports as a percentage of gross national product	10.07	10.46	12.42	12.19	12.72	14.99	19.12	17.93	18.76	19.18	20.0
Exports as a percentage of gross national product	5.53	5.81	6.41	6.17	6.23	7.80	9.77	9.62	9.58	9.27	9.7
Imports as a percentage of gross national product	4.54	4.65	6.00	6.02	6.49	7.19	9.34	8.31	8.82	9.90	10.3

Source: *Statistical Abstract of the United States: 1979* (100th edition) (Washington, D.C.: U.S. Bureau of the Census, 1979).

percent of total imports, more than two-thirds the share of the total represented by all of Western Europe. Western European countries have also increased their exports to the United States in recent years, though more slowly than Japan.

Composition of Imports

The composition of the import sector is as significant as its changing magnitude. We are accustomed to thinking of the United States as a large importer of petroleum and of certain raw materials, including chromium, cobalt, copper, lead, and zinc. We are less accustomed to thinking of the United States as an importer of iron and steel, nonferrous metals, electronic equipment, and other specialized manufactured goods. Yet between 1970 and 1979, imports in each of the product sectors of manufactured goods increased dramatically. Manufactured goods as a proportion of all imports rose from one fourth in 1960 to half of all imports in 1979 (see table 2–18). During the 1976–1978 period of cyclical stability, despite a devalued U.S. dollar, imports of manufactured goods grew markedly, increasing an estimated 120 percent between 1975 and 1979.

Among manufactured products, the largest import increases during the 1970s were imports of nonferrous metals, with iron and steel products a close second. But imports of machinery, transport, and equipment rose by 128 percent between 1975 and 1979 (see table 2–18). Valued at over $53 billion, these imports are products that the United States formerly exported to other countries. We are now importing them for a number of reasons, all discouraging: the price is lower, the quality is better, the product is highly differentiated, or U.S. capacity cannot supply sufficient quantities to meet domestic demand. Imports of other manufactured goods rose 93 percent in this period to over $46 billion.

Import competition clearly reduces domestic employment opportunities. One estimate is that for every $1 billion in trade deficit, 40,000 jobs are eliminated.[7] The incidence of job loss may be greatest on those least able to find other work, such as garment workers in major urban centers like New York or semi-skilled assembly workers in rural areas of the United States like Alabama and South Carolina.

American labor unions have been vocal in their resistance to the export of jobs through import of products. Unions have led the battle for government assistance to workers laid off or let go as a consequence of imports (trade-adjustment assistance). They have lobbied for quotas and tariffs and measures to penalize foreign firms for dumping goods in the United States at below-cost prices. For example, for more than ten years, the International Ladies Garment Workers Union has been in the forefront of efforts

Table 2–18
General Imports and Exports by Selected Commodity Groups, 1960–1979
(millions of dollars)

Item	1960	1965	1970	1975	1979
General exports	20,408	27,178	42,590	106,561	181,801
General imports	15,073	21,427	39,952	96,573	206,326
Food and live animals					
Exports	2,684	4,002	4,356	15,484	22,245
Imports	2,996	3,460	5,375	8,503	15,170
Crude materials, except fuels					
Exports	2,805	2,855	4,605	9,784	20,755
Imports	2,752	3,102	3,307	5,566	10,650
Mineral fuels and related materials					
Exports	842	947	1,595	4,470	5,615
Imports	1,587	2,221	3,075	26,476	60,060
Chemicals					
Exports	1,776	2,403	3,826	8,691	17,306
Imports	807	768	1,450	3,696	7,485
Machinery and transport equipment					
Exports	6,992	10,139	17,882	45,668	70,403
Imports	1,466	2,948	11,172	23,457	53,678
Other manufactured goods					
Exports	3,815	4,890	7,636	16,592	22,657[a]
Imports	4,572	7,528	13,285	23,927	46,299[a]

Source: *Statistical Abstract of the United States: 1979* (100th edition) (Washington, D.C.: U.S. Bureau of the Census, 1979). 1979 data are from the *Survey of Current Business,* Bureau of Economic Analysis, February, 1980.

[a] These data are taken from the *Statistical Abstract of the United States, 1979*, and are for the year 1978.

both to protect American goods from unfair foreign competition and to improve the productivity of American plants.

Other unions, such as steelworkers and autoworkers, have also sought protection from unfair competition but have been less forward-looking in their approach to technological advance, new product design, and efficient production scheduling. Understandably, workers fear technological displacement. Thus, there was no clarion call from labor demanding new convection furnaces or continuous-rolling systems for producing steel in Youngstown until it was too late. But by resisting new technology and increased productivity, labor is writing an advance application for unemployment insurance, because without such efficiencies, it is a foregone conclusion that, ultimately, the plants and firms that cannot compete will have to shut down. It is in labor's long-term self-interest to cooperate with management and government to hasten new efficiencies and to deal with the problem of worker displacement through training, relocation, and severance compensation, rather than through maintenance of unneeded workers in obsolete production environments.

When imports do displace a large number of workers in industries that, for historial reasons, still tend to be heavily concentrated geographically, such as New York's apparel industry, the negative impact of import penetration can be very localized. Youngstown, Ohio, is the classic example of an entire community being devastated by the closing of an antiquated steel plant that could not continue to compete with foreign steel.

The long-term benefits of international trade must not be sacrificed to immediate political concerns, however, and there is a clear danger that this will happen. Understandably concerned with protecting the jobs of its members, organized labor has moved slowly but perceptibly away from its traditional free-trade position. For example, the United Auto Workers Union, reversing a 40-year tradition of advocating free trade, is now leading the drive to restrict imports of automobiles. In 1979 the AFL-CIO vigorously opposed the nomination of two free-trade appointees to the International Trade Commission, the agency with authority to process complaints of domestic producers against foreign imports. The Commission is responsible for determining whether a domestic industry, such as the shoe or textile or steel industry, has been materially harmed by imports demonstrably subsidized by foreign governments or dumped in the United States at prices below their production costs. Unions cannot be faulted for attempting to make existing laws work in the favor of workers. Nevertheless, in the long run, jobs can be preserved only if organized labor helps to solve long-term questions of labor cost and labor productivity. The U.S. economy cannot function for the welfare of all Americans behind permanent trade fortresses.

Trade Imbalances and Sectoral Policies

Altering the nation's trade position depends not merely on trade policy but on increasing the competitive advantage of specific sectors and industries. Monetary, fiscal, regulatory, spatial, and sectoral policies all influence individual firms' ability to maintain markets at home and abroad.

Trade imbalances can be reduced not only by decreasing imports but also by increasing exports. A four-fold increase in exports was realized in the 1970–1979 period (see tables 2–17 and 2–18). Nevertheless, U.S. firms are losing market share abroad in some vital industries.

The declining American share of export markets is due in part to lack of price and quality competitiveness. It is also due, perhaps in larger part, to lack of vigorous effort to develop exports. Since postwar American economic history was, until 1974, one of constantly expanding domestic purchasing power, American firms too often were satisfied with a domestic market. They paid relatively little attention to overseas customers as long as profits were piling up. By contrast, other OECD countries, especially West Germany, France, and Japan, engaged in a wide range of market-developing and market-maintaining practices. Usually, these practices were closely integrated—or are in the process of being integrated—with domestic regional economic-development policies and with micro policies in general. Universally, the policies reflected a conviction that the new structure of capitalism demands a regular, close, stable, visible, and permanent linkage between business and government.

The Japanese example indicates the linkage of export promotion to other economic-development incentives. It is a fundamental responsibility of the Japanese government to encourage industry to compete successfully in world markets and to discourage, even to eliminate, enterprises that show little promise of remaining or becoming competitive. To do this, the Japanese government enters the market in numerous ways: by controlling access to capital and limiting it to high-priority industries; by providing land for new factory construction; by forcing modernization through licensing and financing it through tax breaks; by providing market forecasts for exporting industries that are organized into broad trade sectors; by sponsoring research and development of new products, especially those that might not be currently profitable but offer export potential; by controlling permits for new plants; by subsidizing excess capacity when that is deemed desirable. All of this is accomplished by an interlocking industrial-government bureaucracy with decades of tradition and experience behind it.

The Ministry of International Trade and Industry (MITI) controls prices and can arrange cartels, force modernization or rationalization of firms, and take many other steps to increase efficiency and productivity. These powers enable MITI to protect Japanese firms from sudden or extreme changes in costs of industrial inputs. For example, MITI was able to cushion the inflationary impact of OPEC price increases in 1974 by holding domestic price increases to a lower rate. Subsequently, MITI compensated Japanese oil companies in 1977 by allowing domestic prices to stay high despite the interim appreciation of the yen, which reduced the relative cost of oil imports and, in a free market, would have allowed current prices to fall.

Integrated fiscal and financial policy is a major element of Japanese management of production and trade. Japan's main central bank, Bank of Japan, is supervised by the Ministry of Finance, which also oversees the tax system. Thus the government, through the Ministry of Finance, controls both the cost and distribution of loans and the tax breaks that are offered to selected industries disadvantaged by other governmental policies. As Ezra Vogel, the Harvard-based expert on "Japan, Inc." points out, this fiscal-monetary merger in the government is the basic reason that Japanese industry weathers world market fluctuations successfully. For example, the shipbuilding industry, damaged by the 1971 revaluation of the yen, was given special tax dispensation to compensate for the decreased real value of ship sales.[8]

In Japan, government guidance for the privately owned economy is carried out with the close and regular cooperation of the business community. This is achieved in the main through the Keidanren, a professionally staffed organization representing business and industry. All major policy issues are discussed among MITI, the Keidanren, and other appropriate organizations. The objective is consensus. Disagreements among sectors as to appropriate priorities are thrashed out. Conflicts between larger and smaller firms are debated, and ways to compensate "losers" in a policy decision are often arranged. Dissension is viewed as a necessary stage in a process leading to widespread if not unanimous agreement. But MITI has the last word and final authority.[9]

Although cultural differences and history prohibit the wholesale transfer of the Japanese approach to economic development to the United States, some aspects of the Japanese approach are transferable to our larger, more diffuse, and more loosely organized system without sacrificing the advantages of pluralism. The most important of these aspects is the attitude of mutuality between government and business. The nation's prosperity rests on the prosperity of its economic enterprises and determines the government's ability to provide services and improve the quality of life. Thus government and industry, despite inevitable disagreement as to means, are in total agreement that they are partners, not adversaries, with respect to ends.

A more rational and integrated approach to industry's needs and opportunities is needed in the United States. Export promotion must be a primary ingredient of such an approach. Increased exports would have beneficial effects other than creating new domestic jobs or concentrating them in areas of high unemployment. Federal tax revenues would be increased if exports were achieved without tax subsidies; even if they were encouraged by subsidies, in the long run the differences between subsidies and returns would be calculated to increase net federal revenue. It has been estimated that exports have a federal tax yield of .4 and a domestic multiplier of 2; that is, every $1 billion in exports yields $400 million in taxes and creates $2 billion worth of domestic production.[10]

It is certainly true that, in the interests of worldwide efficiency in production, production will and largely should flow to areas of least cost. But equity must also be considered, and it is not simply a matter of providing jobs for the impoverished workers of the developing and emerging nations. The United States and the other advanced industrial nations have built a society of relative economic equality, of minimal comfort for all citizens and substantial comforts for the majority. They have learned through bitter experience to balance the short-term interests of economic growth and prosperity with concern for conserving and enhancing resources—including the natural environment—over the long term. We cannot allow the worldwide shifts in economic opportunities to destroy the American commitment to quality of life, either at home or overseas.

But trade protectionism, which seems to be surging in other advanced industrial countries as well as in the United States, is no more the answer today than it was in the 1930s. To reserve domestic markets for ourselves, erecting trade barriers against all products and commodities that we want to produce at home, would lead to trade wars. Countries controlling critical raw materials would embargo them to the United States. High tariff or non-tariff fences against manufactures would lead to reciprocal barriers against American goods. Rather than providing economic security, protectionism would fuel inflation, because there would be no incentive to reduce costs to compete with imports; discourage innovation; and unleash disruptive political forces in other countries.

The only other choice is an integrated domestic economic policy that permits firms in the United States to operate on a least-cost basis. Trade policy alone is not enough because if goods cannot be produced domestically at competitive prices, there will be nothing for us to trade. Therefore, measures must be taken jointly by government, labor, and business to remove unnecessary barriers to cost reduction and open up new markets for American goods.

The Myth of a Free Market

A realistic approach to the problem is needed—one that deals with the facts, the prospects, and the costs of achieving a more rational approach to economic development. There is no room for economic romanticism. But many policymakers hold an anachronistic belief in an imaginary free market in which government plays no role. Adam Smith's eighteenth-century description of the capitalistic economy has been outdated for at least a century, but an idealized vision of a highly competitive, magically efficient free market made up of numerous small firms survives with remarkable tenacity. This myth is belied by the facts.

Virtually every basic commodity market is controlled by a relatively small number of firms. In food supply, as Richard Barnet has shown, the world grain market is dominated by three companies, and control of the rice market is also highly centralized. The petroleum market is dominated by the "seven sisters." The gold market, diamond market, silver market, zinc market, and copper market are dependent on the decisions of very few corporate executives. In fact, there is more competition among firms in industries that are regularly scrutinized by the U.S. Justice Department— for example, steel, autos, air frames, electronics, railroads—than in many other key economic endeavors.

World-scale oligopoly is a fact. Nationally and regionally, the urge to manage markets is a realistic response to the complexities of the production and distribution systems and the fast pace of innovation. The interdependency of industries comprising sectors extends over large regions and often is so concentrated that entire communities are vulnerable to collapse if sectoral shifts occur. The pace of technological change is so rapid that many firms cannot absorb new technologies as fast as they are invented. Even if production can be quickly altered, the marketing apparatus can crack under the momentum of new modifications. The contemporary reality is that numerous small competitors cannot absorb the management costs required to operate in fast-paced, supersophisticated world markets. They cannot pay for the accountants, lawyers, technical advisors, advertising people, and other personnel who provide needed support services. Under such conditions, forced competition may lead to multiple bankruptcy. But guided markets with definite output requirements and clear market goals can allocate market shares to individual producers and can provide the support system needed to maintain quality control.

The many dangers associated with international cartelization may be no greater than the danger of pretending that the impulse to control markets can be entirely suppressed. For example, we seldom think about costs to the American taxpayers of pursuing anti-big-business policies in our government (at the same time that European nations have implemented policies to encourage integration, consolidation, and economies of scale). This money could be spent, instead, on social programs or could be returned to taxpayers to be invested or saved—which would ultimately boost the economy. Nor is there much consistency in the United States' stance concerning big business. In 1979, for example, the Justice Department was bringing lawsuits to break up two of the nation's most successful corporations, IBM and ATT, at a time when a third major corporation, Chrysler, on the verge of bankruptcy, was receiving a congressional gift of $1.5 billion in unsecured loans.

In stark contrast to confused American practices, efficient large-scale units are encouraged by the West German, French, and Japanese governments. Should employees or entrepreneurs be disadvantaged by this policy, they are compensated. It is time to look at the advantages offered by scale, by concentration of decision-making, and by at least partial management of markets.

This is not to minimize the fact that small firms offer some major advantages and should be protected from predatory takeovers. The independence that allows for innovation is much to be desired and encouraged. But innovation is more often found in small firms not for reasons related to size per se, but because an inventor or innovator in a large corporation receives neither money nor fame, as a rule, for accomplishment. The patent goes to the corporation, as do all production rights, and any bonus paid the inventor is not generally princely in scale. To encourage innovation, it might be most expedient for large-scale firms, which can absorb the cost of basic or exploratory research, to alter the reward system. Innovation can proceed in large firms as well as in small firms if the payoffs are equal—and better, perhaps, in large ones for those who do not relish the sink-or-swim philosophy.

Of course, the greatest irony of the "Smith myth" is that it perpetuates the illusion that business wishes to operate without government. Nowhere do businessmen complain more about the benefits they actively seek and receive from government than in the United States. Government support of the Lockheed Corporation, Wisconsin Steel, and the Chrysler Corporation exemplifies the extraordinary dependence of business upon government under adverse "free market" circumstances. Business lobbies for incentives, favorable tax treatment, regulations that control market entry, export-import loans, and numerous other ends, spending millions of dollars each year. Much of the lobbying effort, to be sure, is to persuade Congress to remove restrictions and regulations, but considerable effort is spent seeking government intervention and special advantage. The economic reality of our times is that the operations of business and government are inextricably linked.

Notes

1. Gross domestic product is gross national product minus gross product originating outside the nation, such as the value of goods produced and sold overseas.

2. U.S., Department of Commerce, Bureau of Economic Analysis, *Survey of Current Business*. Washington, D.C., Volume 59, Number 6, June 1979, p. 22.

3. Calculated by authors from unpublished data of the U.S. Department of Commerce, Bureau of Economic Analysis.

4. Gail Garfield Schwartz and Pat Choate, *Revitalizing the U.S. Economy: A Brief for National Sectoral Policies*. The Academy for Contemporary Problems, Columbus, Ohio, January 1980, p. 6.

5. U.S., Congress, Senate, Subcommittee on International Finance, Committee on Banking, Housing and Urban Affairs, *Multilateral Trade*

Negotiations (Washington, D.C.: U.S. Government Printing Office, 1979), p. 19.

6. This includes merchandise, goods and services.

7. Stanley H. Ruttenberg, *The Impact of Manufacturing Trade on Employment* (Washington, D.C.: National Commission for Manpower Policy 1978), pp. 1–56.

8. Ezra Vogel, "Guided Free Enterprises in Japan," *Harvard Business Review,* May–June 1978.

9. Ibid.

10. U.S. Congress, Senate, Subcommittee on Finance, Committee on Banking, Housing and Urban Affairs, *Multinational Trade Negotiations,* Hearings, April 4–5 (Washington, D.C.: U.S. Government Printing Office, 1979), p. 17.

3 Selected Industrial and Sectoral Problems

The linkages and interdependencies among industries within major economic divisions are extremely complex. But these interdependencies cross the macro sectors as well, thus obviating the functional significance of dividing the economy into agriculture, forestry, mining, transportation, manufacturing, trade, and services. Manufacturing no longer depends on one or a few basic materials but utilizes many diverse building blocks constructed of combinations of materials in a fashion that is itself a complex process. Plastics are produced from petroleum by-products. Other synthetics are chemically created from fibers and metals. Fusion metals are produced in sheets, plates, ingots, bars, wires, and film from many combinations of base metals and minerals, processed by electromagnetic techniques. These man-made inputs to manufacturing can be suppressed entirely if for some reason one ingredient, such as titanium or magnesium, cannot be had, even if only minute amounts are needed. While technology is continually inventing new products from known ingredients, the very sophistication of the products sometimes introduces instability into the entire chain of operations dependent upon them.

Just as there are intricate interdependencies between manufacturing and agriculture, mining, and forestry, so there are interdependencies between the service activities in the postindustrial economy and the manufacturing sectors. The computerized systems that can monitor and control complex operations, such as the production of electricity, almost without human participation, are no more than manufactured items into which systems analysts and programmers have imprinted intelligence. Thousands of applications of computer technology have yet to be perfected. The simpler, smaller, and cheaper the hardware, the more opportunities are opened up to invent and market the software. The more uses envisioned for applying the available technology, the greater is the incentive to improve quality and reduce cost of the manufactured elements.

As mentioned earlier, these interdependencies are not always geographically limited. While the interindustry linkages in the automotive sector, for historical reasons, are rather heavily concentrated in the Great Lakes states, other industries can be devastated by events taking place thousands of miles away. A manufacturer of plastic toys in New York, for example, can be bankrupted by the lack of cracking capacity in, say, Louisiana to break crude oil into the components that ultimately will give him the raw materials he needs.

Within the sectors consisting of clusters of industries, a component industry is subject to stress in five basic elements in the production process: materials, equipment, energy, labor, and nonproductive costs.

If an industry can't get raw materials at a reasonable price on a certain and regular basis, it is in trouble. "Raw" materials may include manufactured items, if the output of one industry is the input for others.

Having materials on hand is useless to any industry if it doesn't have or can't get the equipment needed to process materials. Equipment may be unobtainable because of excess demand for a particular piece of equipment, creating a market queue; or prohibitive cost; or unavailability of parts or raw materials needed to manufacture it; or lack of financing.

Energy must be available to power the equipment. The higher energy is as a proportion of per-unit production costs, the more critical its price will be. As in the case of raw materials, continuity of supply may be more critical than price for some industries.

To some degree labor may be substituted for energy, but at a cost of delay. On average in all industries, labor is the most costly input to production. Skilled labor is much in demand in many industries, but there is excess labor in others. In some industries as much as one-fourth of all workers may be functionally redundant; still, in some sectors, jobs go begging. The occupational mobility of labor is critical to productivity increases as well as to solving the structural unemployment problem. The pace of technological change may dictate more than one skill shift for every worker in a lifetime. Occupational mobility may require locational mobility, too.

Finally, an industry may have a hard time remaining competitive if it has to spend a large amount of money on activities that do not contribute to the creation of the goods or services it is selling. The expense must be reflected in the price; but if the resulting price is higher than that of similar goods produced under circumstances that do not require the expense, the industry (or certain firms in it) will have trouble disposing of the product at a profit. Expenses that are nonproductive are expenses to maintain the environment; expenses for ensuring health and safety; expenses for ensuring equity in the distribution of jobs, promotions, and fringe benefits among all applicants for them; and expenses to protect the firm against lawsuits, especially consumer complaints and antitrust actions.

The degree to which any of these factors has a negative impact on an industry varies according to a number of factors: what has gone before, what is happening elsewhere, and what is likely to happen in the near future that influences estimates, plans, and investment decisions today. These factors have both a private and a public side. The following sections illustrate the problems faced in particular industries and sectors, and indicate the type of analysis that must be applied in order to determine both *if* and *how* government should assist in avoiding potential disruptions.

Raw Materials

Raw-materials availability is critical to the production chain. Although many industries use semiprocessed materials as inputs, all input costs depend ultimately on the supply and cost of minerals, agricultural and forest products, and their derivatives; and chemical substitutes. Such materials are often made scarce or costly by political as well as economic events. A revolution, or simply the use of trade policy as an instrument of foreign policy, can cut off the supplies of such critical materials as chrome, bauxite, and zinc quickly and indefinitely.

Quantity of minerals and metals is not necessarily their most significant characteristic. The availability of small amounts of one mineral may be more important than the availability of large amounts of another. And in many cases, the quality of the input is the crucial characteristic.

The materials situation is volatile. In 1976 the Congressional Budget Office reported:

> Disturbances in the market for primary commodities are of concern in the U.S. not only because they affect the domestic economy, but also because their effects sometimes extend to the economies of other nations whose interests are allied with our own. The U.S. is rich in many raw materials and has an economy sufficiently diverse to overcome most short-term disruptions.[1]

But in 1980, this view appears overoptimistic, particularly regarding minerals with concentrated production, which are especially vulnerable to political limitations. For example, 91 percent of the world production of chromium comes from South Africa and the USSR; 88 percent of manganese production comes from Australia, Brazil, Africa, and the USSR; chromite comes from Africa, Turkey, and the USSR. Tin, mercury, phosphate, and phosphate rock are similarly found in a few countries. In sum, the United States depends on foreign sources in whole or in part for 22 of the 74 non-energy mineral commodities considered by the Department of Interior as most essential to its economy. The Congressional Budget Office predicts that by 1985 the United States will depend on imports for as much as half of basic supplies of raw materials, which means that the deficit in the mineral balance of trade alone could approach $100 billion by the year 2000. France, Germany, and Japan negotiated agreements with mineral-rich nations to trade access to raw materials for technical assistance. The United States has not done so.

Materials shortages may influence markets for intermediary and final products. For example, if the United States experiences a shortage of chromium, its competitors will not merely seek to export chromium at a high price to the United States. They will also seek to make and export products using the material, following the basic economic dictum to maximize value added through processing.

Manufacturing will naturally flow to mineral-rich countries as they try to develop. As developing nations build their treasuries and gain access to credit, they will increasingly seek to process rather than merely supply materials. For example, Spain is now constructing a large aluminum complex with financing from American banks. In this volatile international context, it is important for the United States to anticipate the competition so that offsets can be planned as appropriate.

Manufacturing

The nature and the role of manufacturing in the United States economy have been changing for almost three decades. Although the overall level of manufacturing activity has risen steadily, the pace of growth has not equaled that of the economy as a whole. Specifically, in 1950 the value added by manufacturing created nearly 30 percent of GNP. By 1978 the value added by manufacturing represented 24 percent of the GNP. Thus, in the span of less than three decades, there was a decline of more than 5 percentage points in manufacturing's contribution to national income.

Both long-term (secular) and short-term (cyclical) forces affect individual industries differently. These differences reflect, among other considerations, the individual industry's maturity, capital/labor intensity, technological superiority, and relative domestic and international competitiveness. The disastrous experience of the steel and auto-assembly industries can be repeated in other industries. As in these industries, competitive failure can lead to plant shutdowns, community stress, and worker dislocation. Future competitive stress will not be limited to low-technology, low-skill-level manufacturing.

Five specific industries now experiencing negative change have been selected to represent a cross-section of sectoral concerns. Steel is a mature, basic, durable-good industry. Aluminum is a young, basic, mixed durable/nondurable-good industry. Apparel is a mature, nondurable-good industry. Semiconductors is a very young, high-growth, high-technology, durable-good industry. Biochemical engineering is an infant industry with still-unimagined growth potential.

Steel

The steel industry has been a problem in the United States economy for more than 20 years. Its competitive position is weak. Because steel is a fundamental element in the durable-goods segment of the economy, weakness in the industry is a source of inflationary pressures. Steel is of course vital to the national defense capability. Moreover, steel is the basic material for some 44 percent of U.S. exports;[2] its price and quality strongly influence the U.S. balance of trade. The recent history of the American steel industry has been one of rising prices, uneven quality, and falling output.

Production in the U.S. steel industry has been declining since 1974. American firms are losing their share of overall world production of steel. The value of steel production exceeded $48 billion in 1979 (see table 3-1). But while in 1950 the United States produced 46 percent of the world's steel, in 1978 it produced only 17 percent of world output. In the period 1950–1978, world steel production expanded 377 percent. Yet U.S. production grew by only 41 percent. U.S. imports of steel increased threefold between 1960 and 1978. In 1960 the United States imported 3.4 million tons of steel, or 5 percent of total domestic consumption. By 1979, U.S. imports had risen to 15 million tons, or almost 14 percent of total U.S. consumption.

Despite falling production, the American steel industry in 1979 employed 451,000 workers. Labor productivity in the steel industry has been growing at a lower rate than that of other industries. In the period 1964–1976, labor productivity in steel expanded at a rate of only 1.4 percent annually. Labor costs of Japanese production are approximately half those in the United States, and the costs of capital construction are also substantially lower. Major technological breakthroughs are needed to increase the United States comparative advantage.

Table 3-1
Steel Mill Products: Vital Statistics, 1974–1979
(millions of dollars)

Item	1974	1976	1978	1979
Value of shipments	34,445	32,762	42,828	48,291
Total employment (000)	512	454	449	451
Value of exports	2,118	1,225	1,329	1,668
Value of imports	5,116	4,025	6,917	6,384

Source: *1980 U.S. Industrial Outlook* (Washington, D.C.: U.S. Department of Commerce, 1980).

In the period from 1973 to mid-1977, the price of finished U.S. steel rose 79 percent, a price increase almost 24 percent greater than that of other major industrial sectors. Prices have risen steeply for almost all steel inputs, including coal, iron ore, and steel scrap, as well as for labor. In the period 1972-1977, coal prices rose 138 percent, iron ore, 76 percent, and steel scrap, 133 percent.[3] Hourly wage costs involved in the production of steel have risen over 90 percent since 1973. Even so, the Council on Wage and Price Stability reports that profits in the steel industry are lower than those of most other major industrial sectors. In 1976 profits were 3.6 percent of sales.

The United States is requiring its steel plants to make substantial investments in necessary but unproductive pollution control and abatement equipment. In 1979 this equaled almost 18 percent of the total capital expenditures of the steel industry.[4] Antipollution requirements are more rigorous for new plants than for old. Thus many of the public regulatory requirements are actually a disincentive to modernization.

The Council on Wage and Price Stability reports that other nations' subsidies to their steel industry average 1 percent of total cost. Thus, even if the United States followed the subsidy system, a very large investment would be needed to make the domestic industry competitive.

The steel industry operates in a political and economic environment that is resistant to quick and easy change. Despite government financial assistance and protection gained after the crisis of 1977, the steel industry is still unstable, and its potential for structural adaptation is of vital concern to the future of the national economy. But as the Council on Wage and Price Stability reported in October 1977, "no single factor can be identified as responsible for the industry's difficulties, and no single action by the government, the companies or the workers can solve them."

A basic task for the steel industry is to determine which of the principal cost pressures forcing steel prices up will abate. It is necessary to identify all the factors inhibiting the comparative advantage of U.S. firms. If foreign manufacturers' capital and labor costs are lower, and technology is widely diffused, what changes can American government and industry make to bring U.S. production costs into competitive alignment? Japan is able to produce steel on a world-market scale in part because of its economies of scale—is the size of U.S. plants uneconomical? Can U.S. firms attract sufficient capital to operate on a scale appropriate to conditions of world competition? If not, what measures are needed to make this possible?

Regulatory standards required of the steel industry should be reviewed in the light of the industry's importance to the overall economy, including the nation's strategic position. Innovative approaches to environmental protection, such as the "bubble" concept, which would allow plants to offset specific environmental improvements with other, approved emissions, can benefit the industry. But they must be implemented, not merely discussed. Streamlining other regulatory enforcement is possible, particularly for water-pollution standards. Regulations affecting industries on which steel depends, such as coal mining, should be efficiently enforced without wasted paperwork and reporting.

Finally, a policy for the steel industry must examine the issues of pricing and protection. The steel companies seek a government "trigger" price, or import quotas, or both, while they undertake a massive reinvestment strategy. The industry argues that the many government subsidies available to competitive producers overseas, whether or not they are partially owned by foreign governments, put the domestic industry at a price disadvantage in world markets. Among these subsidies are low freight costs, high ratios of debt to equity, easy financing terms, and support of production levels even during times of slack demand. The price of foreign steel sold in the United States, the steel industry argues, should reflect the true cost of these and other inputs in a free-market economy. However, as the Iron and Steel Institute points out, to quantify these values would be very difficult. Measuring them would itself add to the cost of marketing American steel if the steel producers were to do it. Thus a dilemma exists to which there is only one possible answer: government, management, and labor must work on reducing the production costs of American steel. The possibility of public subsidies during a period of transition to higher efficiency must be considered. But subsidies should be contingent on basic changes within the industry.

Aluminum

The aluminum industry has a high growth potential. It employs approximately 231,000 workers at high wage levels (see table 3-2). It provides vital inputs to other manufacturing industries and sectors, particularly aircraft and automotive products. But American firms have not expanded their productive capacity enough to keep up with the growing demand. As a result, the United States imports a growing proportion of its aluminum requirements.

Aluminum is used in building and construction, transportation equipment, including aerospace and automotive equipment, and packaging. It has potential for use in solar heating systems. The light weight and malleability of aluminum have in recent years been complemented by alloy modifications and other fabricating techniques that have increased its strength. This makes it an excellent substitute for steel in motor vehicles and aircraft, and demand from these sectors is expected to grow. Aggregate levels of domestic demand will depend largely on the ability of automobile

Table 3–2
Aluminum: Vital Statistics, 1974–1979
(millions of dollars)

Item	1974	1976	1978	1979
Value of shipments	10,300	10,934	15,829	17,760
Total employment (000)	203	194	220	231
Capital expenditures	490	454	NA	NA
Value of exports	491	493	575	799
Value of imports	383	555	1,118	1,041

Source: *1980 U.S. Industrial Outlook* (Washington, D.C.: U.S. Department of Commerce, 1980).

manufacturers to compete with foreign cars. Aluminum fabrication is expected to grow faster than the economy as a whole until 1984 at least.

The aluminum industry is highly concentrated. Although there are 12 companies engaged in primary aluminum and 69 companies producing secondary ingots, three companies dominate the market.

The major barriers to expansion of aluminum production in the United States have been its dependence on imported bauxite, its high consumption of energy, and a lack of new capital investment. These factors are inter-related, particularly the last two. The industry, formerly dependent on hydroelectric power, now uses oil-, nuclear-, and coal-fired power too. Many firms face large increases in the cost of energy when current supply contracts expire. The fear of disruption in the energy supply has inhibited investment in modern fabrication facilities that could reduce energy consumption by about 25 percent. Therefore, assured energy supply would encourage new investment and more energy-efficient production.

Some government-industry cooperative efforts to deal with the industry's problems are under way. The Federal Department of Energy and Kaiser Aluminum jointly funded a program to develop a smelting process using a coal-fired blast furnace. Legislation to establish a Pacific Northwest regional energy system that would have a major impact on the long-term stability of the aluminum plants in that region was introduced in Congress in 1979. Another proposal for reducing the cost of energy for the aluminum industry is converting oil-fueled plants to coal-fired plants. However, an official of Kaiser Aluminum, one of the highest energy consumers, has testified that even raising the price of oil to twice its 1977 price would not make retrofitting for oil conservation profitable for the company.[5]

Potential disruptions of or price increases in the supply of bauxite are another concern to the industry. Jamaica, Guinea, and Surinam are the major suppliers of bauxite, which is produced in the United States only in

Arkansas, Alabama, and Georgia. U.S. reserves are insufficient to offer the possibility of self-sufficiency in bauxite. The U.S. Bureau of Mines and major aluminum producers are experimenting with aluminum production based on domestic alternatives to bauxite, including clays, alunite, anorthosite, and dawsonite. If such replacements are not found, it is quite possible that the continued industrialization of the bauxite-producing nations will undermine the U.S. producers' supply of the mineral. As those countries increase their capacity to produce intermediate and final products, they will compete with the United States in world markets and perhaps in the United States as well. U.S. imports of alumina have increased steadily over the past few years, principally as a result of the increased processing capacity of Australia, Jamaica, and Surinam.

Aluminum companies carry large long-term debt. The three largest producers are strong enough to secure capital for expansion of plant and equipment if profit projections look promising. It is in the interests of the national economy as a whole to help the industry reduce its energy requirements, find economic substitutes for precarious imported raw materials, and encourage price competitiveness in the domestic industry.

Apparel

The apparel sector is the single largest labor-intensive sector in the United States. Its approximately 1.3 million workers represent almost 9 percent of all production workers in the country (see table 3–3). Garment manufacture is one of the major opportunities for entry-level employment for the unskilled that provides on-the-job training to enable workers to become semiskilled. Over 80 percent of the work force is women; they represent 17 percent of all female manufacturing workers.

Table 3–3
Apparel and Other Textile Products: Vital Statistics, 1974–1979
(millions of dollars)

Item	1974	1976	1978	1979
Value of shipments	30,632	34,759	43,215	46,690
Total employment (000)	1,316.7	1,270.5	1,334.3	1,313.1
Capital expenditures	391.4	422.7	—	—
Value of exports	332.7	434.2	551.0	819.0
Value of imports	2,095.4	3,256.5	4,833.3	5,075.0

Source: *1980 U.S. Industrial Outlook* (Washington, D.C.: U.S. Department of Commerce, 1980).

The apparel sector underwent a period of restructuring during the 1960s and 1970s. As a result, fewer plants exist now than did ten years ago. To achieve production economies, many activities besides the actual sewing of garments were integrated into new factories. Industries such as button-making or thread-making, which in former years were outside but supportive of apparel manufacture, were absorbed by large national-scale operations. New technologies, such as cutting garments with lasers, were introduced. These changes increased apparel-manufacture efficiency and labor productivity.

During the period of restructuring, apparel plants dispersed from their previous locations in Northeast cities. But even in dispersal, the apparel sector remained relatively highly concentrated. Over 70 percent of the work force is in eight states—New York, Pennsylvania, California, North Carolina, New Jersey, Georgia, Texas, and Tennessee.

Apparel manufacture is sensitive to the ups and downs of the business cycle, and the number of apparel-sector jobs fluctuates rather sharply. New technology has allowed wages in this traditionally low-wage sector to rise a bit, but most of the labor requirement is in the sewing, and technology has increased sewing productivity only marginally since the invention of the modern sewing machine.

There is little prospect for major job expansion or substantially higher wages in the industry. Apparel manufacture is easily installed in any country, and low-wage foreign labor competes effectively against the capital-intensive American firms in many of the industries that comprise the apparel sector. But because these industries are highly differentiated by type and quality of garment, the entire sector is volatile, and some components are more sensitive to import competition than others. In 1979 almost $5.1 billion of apparel was imported to the United States. This represented a 142-percent increase over 1974, when imports were valued at $2.1 billion. Exports of United States-made apparel, of course, have not kept pace. In 1974, the U.S. exported $.3 billion of apparel; in 1979, $.8 billion.

Apparel imports are increasing despite protection given to garment manufacture by the Arrangement Regarding International Trade in Textiles (Multifiber Arrangement) with 17 leading supplying countries. In a competitive world market, the limited scope for reducing labor intensity, the high cost of U.S. labor, and the ease of market entry for firms in developing nations ensure that the apparel sector will continue to erode. The issue therefore will be how to cushion the impact of declining apparel sales on domestic workers and the communities where they live. Interventionist policy choices include trade-adjustment assistance, sectoral subsidies, and trade barriers. Another choice is not to intervene and to let economics take their natural course, while assisting garment workers to find other employment.

The Semiconductor Industry

Semiconductors are critical to an amazing number of industries and sectors. Semiconductors are used in radios, televisions, calculators, communications equipment, automotive products, and industrial and environmental-control systems of all varieties. The importance of semiconductors to other sectors is indicated by the fact that the industry is now annually shipping $6 billion of products that are incorporated into more than $200 billion of goods and services in other manufacturing and communications industries. The world semiconductor market is expected to pass the $20 billion level by 1985. The American-owned semiconductor industry employs approximately 185,000 workers. Almost 85,000 are offshore workers.[6]

In September 1979 the U.S. Department of Commerce, Industry and Trade Administration, released a study that noted a decline in the U.S. share of the semiconductor market. During the decade of the 1970s, Japan, Taiwan, and West Germany progressively expanded their production base and marketing activities. Some of this overseas growth is directly due to offshore U.S. investments. Because semiconductor manufacturing is labor-intensive, U.S. manufacturers have sought overseas labor, which is less costly. However, much more of this expansion is the consequence of investments by foreign-owned firms.

The introduction of the integrated circuit eliminated much of the distinction between the makers of electronic components and the equipment producers. Integrated circuits have made it both technically and economically feasible to vertically integrate manufacturing and to produce both components and end products. Thus firms such as Texas Instruments now produce not only components but products, such as wristwatches and hand-held calculators, that use these components. Automobile manufacturers are either bringing semiconductors into their own facilities or contracting for sure supplies. The economies of vertical integration plus rising capital costs, lack of equity capital, and rising R&D expenditures have encouraged take-overs of independents by large corporations, reduced the entry of new small firms into this industry, and made competitive conditions for remaining small firms difficult.

The application of advanced solid-state technology to commercial semiconductor producers requires a continuing research and development effort. In the past, research in this area was supported by government funding of space and military investments. During the past decade, both the industry and government have reduced their relative levels of support for these R&D efforts.

In the wide array of electronic hardware and software industries, technological advances lead rapidly to new product-generations. The rapid obsolescence of previous generations of equipment is a driving force in many computer-dependent operations. Every breakthrough has enormous potential in terms of market share; for example, a new microchip that multiplies memory capacity creates a demand for entire new computer systems. These technological advances have also made possible constant decreases in production costs as markets expand.

Because the semiconductor industry is a basic component of an advanced industrial nation's economic base, foreign governments have taken steps to enable their nationals to become competitive on a world scale. The Japanese government, for example, sponsors an effort called the Very-Large-Scale Intergrated Circuit Program (VLSI). This program combines the resources and talents of five major Japanese electronic companies to develop competitive technology in microelectronic devices. Japanese firms captured nearly half the integrated-circuit market in 1979 and doubled their shipments to the United States over 1978 levels, according to the U.S. Department of Commerce (see figure 3-1). Other nations, such as the United Kingdom, France, and Germany, are also creating government programs to enhance their semiconductor capacities.

The U.S. government will ignore these trends at peril. Currently government neither explicitly hinders nor helps the domestic semiconductor industry, except for limited trade-adjustment assistance for firms and workers materially harmed by imports. But the importance of the semiconductor industry for America's future world competitive advantage testifies to the need for further assistance.

Many institutional complexities must be considered. The future of the American semiconductor industry may require restrictions on mergers and acquisitions. However, maintaining international competitiveness may require intervention designed to bolster small firms or even subsidize new entrants to the electronics market. Oligopoly has proved to be a drag on innovation in the auto sector and others. Given the innovative role that small electronics firms have exerted in the past, should efforts be made, even at a cost to efficiency, to encourage new start-ups of small firms? Or should policy encourage consolidation and support innovation in the larger firms? For government, business, and labor it is important to consider these questions in the context of likely opportunities and shifts in international markets in the short and long terms.

Biochemicals

In contrast to the declining sectors and the transitional semiconductor industry, the biochemical sector is new-born and likely to boom. The 1980 Supreme Court decision allowing the patenting of processes that combine or recombine natural elements to produce man-made matter opened the door

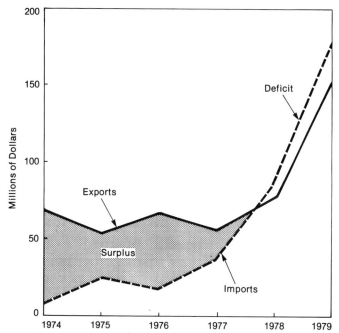

Source: *1980 U.S. Industrial Outlook* (Washington, D.C.: U.S. Department of Commerce, 1980).

Figure 3–1. Integrated-Circuit Trade with Japan

to a whole new world of scientific industries. Recombinant DNA tech-niques, or gene splicing, have so far produced three substances—human insulin, human growth hormone, and human interferon—that promise many applications and will undoubtedly lead to further applications of eso-teric biology, all of which will have commercial possibilities. The over-the-counter securities market has done a rapid trade in the equities of com-panies in the biological-engineering business; venture capital, though still low at about $150 million in 1980, is increasing rapidly.[7]

The uses to which recombinant substances can be put are many, and demand will come from the health industries, the petrochemicals sector—for example, using bacteria to "eat up" oil spills and, perhaps, to "drink" oil from shale—agriculture, and other sectors. Just one new system for bio-logically producing industrial chemicals and thylene derivatives has a huge potential world market for plastics. Other biological industries are not based on gene splicing but involve "contrived" enzymes and antibodies.

The biological industries are presently regulated by the National Insti-tutes of Health in accordance with federal guidelines restricting the amount of production of any single product if research is funded by the federal government, as most genetic research is. Private-industry scientists, though not bound by the regulations, have generally followed the guidelines. Although only 12 of the 191 research centers registered by the National Institutes of Health are commercial centers, more commercial research can certainly be expected.

The danger to watch for is a repetition of occurrences that have marked other technological breakthroughs when they reached the production stage. One is the possibility that commercial ventures will license foreign operators to produce commercial products outside of the United States, thus effectively preventing the U.S. economy from benefiting from the technical, packaging, and distribution jobs. Licensing of bioproducts invented or made practicable with public-sector research support should be accomplished on terms compatible with both national production goals and international trade objectives, and the government has an interest in seeing that this happens.

The other major danger is the possibility of monopolistic control of products or processes that keep them off the market or raise their price beyond the point where they can be widely used. It would be reasonable to expect a pattern similar to that which is emerging in the electronics industry; that is, as soon as a process or product or technique becomes critical to another "user" industry, large firms in that industry will try to buy out the smaller, innovative ventures. Whether or not this will have a long-term negative effect on price or availability or will depress new innovation is a legitimate public concern. The nation should not wait for potential antitrust actions to address the issue. For substances as important to human health and prosperity as these new life-creating techniques, ordinary patent laws should not apply without careful protection of the public interest. Congressional action is needed in this area. Because the issues are so complex, involving antitrust laws, scientific and technological options, and international market conditions, Congress cannot be expected to make informed judgments without considerable review of the issues. A presidential commission on biochemical industries would be an appropriate body to discuss the opportunities in the relevant industries, the capital needs of the industries, the role of product-safety regulations, the role of trade and trade barriers, the role of overseas investment and productions, and the antitrust implications.

Services

Private service-sector growth outpaces manufacturing-sector growth in all the advanced industrial countries. These services include services to individuals, or personal services; the hospitality sector; entertainment; and business and professional services. In the last group, it is the "high" services that will be of particular importance to future economies. These are the activities that have as their clients other businesses or public agencies rather than individuals. The high services include banking, commercial insurance, public relations, investment finance, attorneys, accountants, advertising, planners, advisers, and consultants of various kinds. Communications experts, market-research analysts, pollsters, and even public-policy analysts are all members of the high-service sector. Although the high services are sometimes performed internally in a corporation, they are also purchased from specialists outside the company. (If they are internal to the company, they are staff rather than line positions; they do not contribute directly to the development of, production of, or sales and distribution of the product, but benefit the institution, expand its general market, and contribute to management efficiency.)

High-service activity requires a high level of technical sophistication and skills in problem-solving, negotiation, teamwork, group dynamics, and communications. High-service experts typically work with several people or interest groups having conflicting goals. The high services become more important as society becomes more complex, since more steps are required to make and implement decisions and more actors are involved in doing so. For example, proliferation of performance standards for industry creates a need for technical and legal advice as to how to meet them—or how to legally avoid meeting them—and financial advice on how to treat the cost of doing so.

The high services are an international growth sector. Developing countries as well as advanced countries require these services. As developing nations experiment with fast-track growth, it will be essential to anticipate problems in order to avoid disastrous mistakes. As markets and economies become increasingly interdependent, more and more laws and regulations become relevant, and experts are needed to comprehend and interpret them. The more highly educated societies will naturally be able to provide the largest proportion of the high-service personnel, and for this function the United States offers high-caliber candidates.

Current U.S. dominance in the international services market is reflected in the fact that services are now a major component of the U.S. export base. Between 1970 and 1977, exports of services other than receipts of income on U.S. assets abroad rose 192 percent, from $8,034 million to $24,451 million.[8]

Since the United States may face difficulty in preserving its market share in industries that are, comparatively speaking, heavy users of unskilled and semiskilled labor, it is reasonable to anticipate that the high services will become a larger proportion of total jobs in the United States in the future.[9] Unfortunately, few statistics are available to measure the importance of the high services as a component of the national economic base. A report prepared for the mayor of New York City noted that the high services were a major growth sector, comprising an estimated 65 percent of employment in business services, finance, insurance, and real-estate industries.[10]

Advertising

Advertising employs about 148,000 people and in 1979 registered expenditures of about $49 billion (see table 3-4). Of this, somewhat less than 45 percent represents advertising agency billings. The advertising business in the last three years has been on the upswing, following a decline in the early part of the decade (in real-dollar terms). In 1976 and 1979, the business had record-breaking sales. Large increases in advertising expenditures reflected stiff competition for market shares, as well as a response to an improving economy and rising consumer expenditures.

The advertising industry is moderately concentrated, with nearly 60 percent of billings accounted for by the 72 largest agencies. These agencies employ one-fourth of the advertising work force.

Overseas operations were substantial in 1978, the latest year for which data are available. A survey conducted by *Advertising Age* reported that the 10 largest agencies received $732 million from overseas—almost half their gross income. Rising sales are projected for the future, owing in large part to the continued expansion of the activities of major U.S. multinational corporations into foreign markets with continued reliance on their home-based agency service. It is estimated that advertising expenditures will grow at an annual average rate of 8 percent through 1978-1983.

The advertising business, like other high services, returns to the United States profits generated by the overseas activities of other American-owned

Table 3-4
Advertising: Vital Statistics, 1974-1979
(millions of dollars)

Item	1974	1976	1978	1979
Expenditures	26,740	33,720	43,740	48,940
Total employment (000)	123.8	124.9	141.1	148.3

Source: *1980 U.S. Industrial Outlook* (Washington, D.C.: U.S. Department of Commerce, 1980).

corporations, as well as earning export dollars from foreign clients. In the future, such service activities will become increasingly important to maintain equilibrium in the U.S. balance of payments. At present, no consistent effort is made by either the advertising industry or the federal government to understand the linkages between high-service industries and other sectors, or to estimate accurately the export value of the high-service sector and its economic importance to the nation as a whole or to localities in particular.

Notes

1. U.S., Congress, Congressional Budget Office, *U.S. Raw Materials Policy: Problems and Possible Solutions,* (Washington, D.C.: U.S. Government Printing Office, 1976), p. 1.

2. Steel Tripartite Advisory Committee, "Report of the Working Group on Technological Research and Development," June 1980, Mimeographed, p. 1.

3. Council on Wage and Price Stability, *Prices and Costs in the United States Steel Industry.* Washington, D.C., October 1977, pp. 27–38.

4. U.S., Department of Commerce, Bureau of Economic Analysis, *Survey of Current Business,* vol. 59, no. 2 (Washington, D.C.: U.S. Government Printing Office, February 1979), p. 15.

5. Richard B. Pool, "Applications of Technology to Industrial Processes for Energy Conservation," *Energy Technology IV* (Washington, D.C.: Government Institutes, Inc., 1977), p. 242.

6. U.S., Department of Commerce, *The U.S. Semi Conductor Industry* (Washington, D.C.: U.S. Government Printing Office, 1979), p. 1.

7. Harold M. Schmeck, Jr., "Advances in Gene Splicing Hint Scientific-Industrial Revolution," *The New York Times,* January 27, 1980.

8. *Survey of Current Business,* "Current Business Statistics," June 1979 and June 1980; "General Business Indicators," Quarterly Series.

9. Services constituted 46 percent of national income and product in 1978 ($862.8 billion); a very large proportion of that value was in high services rather than in personal services. Ibid.

10. Gail Garfield Schwartz, "Five Year Recovery Plan," Working Documents, October 1976, New York City Planning Department.

4 Public Intervention in the Economy

Soon after the creation of the United States, the principle was established that government has both the right and the responsibility to intervene in a private free-market economy to serve the general public interest. Since then, of course, the definition of the public interest has been broadened considerably by legislation and by the courts. Legitimate public concerns for which corporate and individual rights may be curtailed include regulating rates and tariffs, regulating entry and exit of firms from specific markets, establishing product and service standards, controlling distribution of critical materials, maintaining safety standards for workers, ensuring fairness in the distribution of jobs and training opportunities, preserving natural resources for multiple purposes (including future economic use), and maintaining the ecology and the environment.

During the last years of the 1970s, many observers began to blame America's economic woes on excessive regulation. A bipartisan push to deregulate the transportation sectors was the strongest manifestation of this sentiment, leading first to the easing of controls on airlines, followed by efforts to lift rate restrictions for the trucking industry. These reforms were undoubtedly needed, although the results may not be the much lower rates and much improved service hoped for.

However, to expect deregulation to solve the country's economic problems is simplistic. Regulation is only one aspect of government intervention in the economy, and while it affects some sectors greatly, it affects others, such as the electronics industry, very little. *All* public intervention affects some or many sectors and industries. The problem is that the sum of the parts is chaos. Much or most intervention is made without regard to the consequences for economic conditions. Because public intervention in the economy is not directed to any performance goals for the economy as a whole, it often produces unanticipated and undesirable side effects. Government rules often work at cross-purposes. The confusing blizzard of government requirements often has no clear purpose. The failure to identify interdependencies among interventions and to assess their cumulative effect is the basic cause for the seemingly disruptive influence of the government in the economic sphere.

For many years U.S. economic policy was nominally based on the economics of Sir John Maynard Keynes. The basic principle of Keynesian policy is that by government manipulating aggregate demand, the economy can be kept on an even keel, avoiding both severe recession and severe inflation. If the economy "overheats" and demand soars to the point where it generates high inflation rates, government cools the economy by restricting the supply of money and credit, increasing its cost, and/or reducing purchasing power through taxation. In times of sluggish demand, government "primes the pump" to get goods and services into circulation and increase investment by opposite measures: lowering the cost of credit, increasing government spending, and expanding purchasing power through tax reductions. The fiscal and monetary manipulations—or macro policy—made by government vary according to specific political and economic circumstances, but the basic thrust of "demand-side" policies remained intact for four decades.

During the 1970s, we came to see that our applications of Keynesian theory failed to work. In 1973–1975 we had recession and inflation simultaneously. We christened this unique situation "stagflation." While prices for goods rose, production declined or remained stagnant. Unemployment rose, too, but most wages did not fall, as theory said they should. Faced with excess capacity, industries failed to reinvest in new equipment, even though credit was obtainable at reasonable cost.

Many reasons can be cited for the continuation of so-called cost-push inflation. Obviously OPEC-controlled oil prices are a major contributor. Add to this the uncertainty of domestic energy supplies. Institutional control has been blamed. Unions protect wages; management protects profits. The cushion of social security, unemployment insurance, and other social programs allows labor to react slowly to demands for wage-control. Government directly supports higher prices for critical materials and goods, such as food. Some analysts attribute responsibility to multinational corporate Machiavellianism.

In reaction to the failure of demand-side policy, many policymakers have become enchanted with its polar opposite; they are now "supply-side" cheerleaders. The solutions of the supply-side economists are simply measures to increase capital investment, which they see as the single obstacle to increased productivity. And increased productivity is the only requirement for improving the U.S. economy, according to the supply-side theorists.

But a narrow, capital-based, supply-side approach would be as impotent as the demand-side approach. It fails to discriminate among the factors that cause different industries to lose competitive advantage. Worse, it fails to define the problem correctly: the problem is to increase markets *and* improve productivity.

Both macro interventions—that is, fiscal and monetary policies—and micro interventions, which are targeted to areas, groups, and classes of activity, must simultaneously be brought to bear on these problems. Our general overall national economic objectives must be measured in terms of output, employment, price stability, and efficiency. The interaction between macro policies and more specific or micro policies is the key to the solution of the problems we now face. Micro interventions such as distressed-area assistance programs, trade control, manpower programs, firm and worker programs under the Trade Adjustment Assistance Act of 1974, small-business assistance, industrial programs such as the Steel Assistance Program, and specially legislated assistance to specific firms, such as the Lockheed and Chrysler aid, can fail or flourish according to the degree that they work with or against macro policy.

And finally, the impact of regulatory activities that have both macro and micro dimensions must be evaluated in terms of the overall economic goals. Regulations affect some industries and sectors differently or more harshly than others. They affect particular places differently than others.

All these interventions, of course, are geared to intended outcomes, which are sometimes achieved. Often, however, the interventions also have unintended outcomes—and these may be more deleterious to general prosperity than the problems originally treated. The only way to prevent such consequences is to understand the cumulative impact of all relevant policies on each major component of the economy.

Fiscal Policy

The government's primary long-term influence on all sectors in the economy lies in its taxing and expenditures powers. Fiscal policies affect individual sectors, industries, and firms differently. The extent of this influence was estimated in 1975 in a series of studies commissioned by the Joint Economic Committee of the Congress (JEC), *Federal Subsidies to Business*. The term *subsidy* was defined very broadly as "the provision of federal economic assistance, at the expense of others in the economy, to private sector producers or consumers of a particular good, service, or factor of production"—a definition we question as being somewhat too sweeping. Although this study, now outdated, underestimates the current influences of tax and expenditure policies of government, it does provide a useful framework for evaluating the effects of federal fiscal policies on business and industry.

Four distinct types of subsidy were distinguished in the JEC study:

1. Direct cash payment, such as a payment by an agency of federal, state, or local government to a private firm or individual in accordance with terms specified by law;
2. Tax subsidy—a reduction in tax liability or a tax credit allowed to an individual or a firm that engaged in specified economic activity, such as purchase of new equipment;

3. Credit subsidy—a government write-down of borrowing costs by guarantee of repayment or participation in a loan transaction to lower the
   rate of interest below what the borrower would otherwise have to pay;
4. Benefit-in-kind subsidies—government sale to private firms or individuals of a good or service at a price below market value (or below cost in
   cases where no private market exists).

In 1975 the total value to business of these four types of government
subsidies was over $95 billion—an increase of nearly 47 percent over the
1971 level of $64.4 billion (see table 4-1). Some industries and sectors bene-
fited substantially more than others. For example, in 1975 the federal government's tax and expenditure subsidies to the transportation sector totalled
$2.3 billion, while subsidies of $15.7 billion went to the housing sector
(including subsidies to buyers through credit mechanisms).

Two known sources of fiscal impact on industrial productivity are the
capital-gains tax and depreciation schedules. These two elements of the tax
code are subject to periodic revisions to balance revenue needs against taxpayers' needs. In theory, the lower the tax on capital, the more investment
will be encouraged. In 1978 Congress reduced the tax on capital gains from
50 percent of the tax rate on wage and salary and fee income to 28 percent, a
reduction of about 20 percent. Econometric forecasters predicted increases
in capital formation of 20 to 40 percent, since interest rates presumably
would fall in response to the increased potential return on equity, the stock
market would rise, and equity capital would flow more readily to corporate
investment. Instead, interest rates soared and the Dow Jones average fell
precipitously. This does not say that the changes in the tax laws were
responsible for rising interest rates or plummeting stock prices, merely that
relationships between the capital markets and the capital-gains tax rates are
not so elementary as some believe.

Across-the-board changes in tax treatment do not necessarily induce
capital to move where it is needed for production purposes. For example,
real-estate tax shelters, which allow ordinary income to be converted into
capital gains and then allow the capital-gains tax to be decreased through
depreciation allowances, has diverted capital from investment in primary
goods, plant, and equipment to investment in social frills, such as vacation
condominiums. Although no study exists to quantify this diversion, for
many ordinary citizens, and for wealthy persons as well, real-estate investments are even less risky than other sheltered investments in production,
such as oil wells or cattle feeding or equities in corporations whose value is
subject to the vagaries of an erratic securities market.

A recent proposal for encouraging new capital investment is the Capital
Cost Recovery Act, colloquially called "10-5-3." This bill would allow
faster depreciation of all business assets. Buildings would be assumed to

Table 4-1
Summary of Federal Subsidy Costs
(billions of dollars)

	Direct Cash Subsidies		Tax Subsidies		Credit Subsidies		Benefit-in-Kind Subsidies		Total Order of Magnitude [a]	
	1970	1975	1970	1975	1970	1975	1970	1975	1970	1975
Agriculture	4.4	0.6	0.9	1.1	0.4	0.7			5.7	2.5
Food		.6	3.2	5.8			1.5	5.9	1.5	5.9
Health	.8	3.3		.7			4.6	10.2	8.6	16.6
Manpower	2.0	5.0	.6	1.0		.1	.1	.4	2.6	4.1
Education	1.9		.8	1.5	.1	.9	.4		3.2	6.5
International	.1		.3		.6				1.0	2.4
Housing	.1	1.7	8.7	12.9	3.0	1.1			11.7	15.7
Natural resources	.1	.1	2.0	4.1			.1		2.1	4.4
Transportation	.3	.6		.1			.2	1.7	.5	2.3
Commerce	2.0	.3	14.1	19.3			1.8	1.9	18.0	21.5
Other			9.4	13.1	.1	.1			9.5	13.2
Total order of magnitude	11.6	12.3	39.9	59.7	4.1	2.9	8.8	20.2	64.4	95.1

Source: Joint Economic Committee of the United States Congress, *Federal Subsidy Programs*, Washington, D.C., 1974.

[a] Individual items may not add to totals due to rounding error.

have a maximum "useful" life of ten years; the maximum useful life of equipment would be set at five years, and the maximum useful life for cars and trucks would be set at three years. This bill would also expand existing tax credits for new investment. The U.S. Treasury Department estimated that the (Jones-Conable) bill would reduce the federal coffers by about $35 billion after four years (in 1984), and after 1989 by twice that amount annually.

Opponents of this bill argue that it is a gift to business, the equivalent of a tax-free loan from the government. Proponents argue that it would increase revenues in the long run by raising productivity and ultimately contributing to higher gross tax receipts from individuals and corporations, even though the tax rates are lower. But neither opponents nor proponents have considered whether this or similar across-the-board tax incentives would encourage the flow of capital into those vital industries that need it the most in order to modernize and ultimately become more productive. The historical precedents would suggest the opposite.

It is also questionable whether across-the-board tax cuts will induce investment in production equipment in a time when capacity utilization in all industrial sectors is at the lowest point since the recession of 1975. However, even in the up-cycles, capacity utilization has not exceeded 85 percent since 1973 and hovered around 80 percent from the end of 1975 to the end of 1977. Capacity ratios vary sector by sector and within sectors as well. Plants producing one kind of steel product may achieve a much higher capacity-utilization ratio than plants producing another steel product. Still, if the capital needs of key sectors are to be met, it would seem appropriate to compare them to capacity-utilization rates, so that the probable impact of tax cuts or specific investment credits can more readily be assessed.

The effect of capital cost-recovery proposals on specific industries will be felt most heavily in some specific places—another consideration should be taken into account before legislation is passed. Accelerated depreciation of buildings and equipment regardless of where they are placed would tend to hasten the abandonment of older factories located in the urban areas and would encourage construction of factories and offices located on cheaper land outside urban areas—thus contributing to urban decline, energy wasted in commuting, and other costs of a dispersed settlement pattern.

The nation has a choice with regard to how tax policies contribute to revitalizing the economy. Although it is true that a completely neutral tax system that had no effect on the allocation of capital would allow capital to flow to the uses of highest productivity, it is equally true that it is economic fantasy to imagine that such a system could exist in the United States. Our tax system, like all other public policies, responds to the pressures of organized economic interests. Taxes *are* an instrument of public policy. Moreover, tax policy *must* be an instrument of public policy in a capitalistic society, because it is the primary lever with which government can induce a privately owned production system to produce socially desirable goods. Without tax policies, for example, we would not have low-income housing, because the return on investment possible at low rents does not attract the needed capital. Without tax policies, many farmers would be bankrupt. Whether too many or too few incentives are directed to each sector is basically a political issue; economists can only illuminate the costs to society of diverting capital from one sector to another.

The problem is not that fiscal subsidies are legislated. It is that no one knows how the subsidies influence key business sectors. No adequate investigation of the sectoral distribution of subsidies has ever been made. It is known, of course, that very risky activities, such as wildcat oil-drilling or cattle-feeding operations, would not be so attractive to investors were it not for advantageous tax treatment. But individual fiscal incentives that channel investment to particular activities should be purposeful. The cumulative impact of many subsidies should be assessed. Both the negative and the positive outcomes of fiscal policy should be reviewed, and reviewed over a considerable time, because short-term and long-term effects will differ by industry.

Monetary Policy

Monetary policy is the major short-term federal economic tool. As the responsibility of the Federal Reserve Board, monetary policy is conceived and administered independently of fiscal policy, trade policy, or other micro policies. The independent Fed theoretically operates with only very general political guidance. Monetary controls are more often than not implemented without regard to their different impacts on different industries and sectors of the economy. Added to the reality that even the overall force of monetary policies is imperfectly understood, this is a disturbing situation. In addition to a better understanding of the effect of tight money on overall prices, investment, and employment, we need to know more about sector-specific effects. In other words, we need to recognize that monetary policy has distributional impacts as well as aggregate impacts.

We have some clues to distributional outcomes. For example, tight money usually diverts investment away from high-risk placements and away from small enterprise. Immediate effects of tight money include drastic curtailment of private construction, especially private housing. The usual political response is either to treat the construction industry to a credit subsidy or to legislate a massive public-works program to take up the slack in construction employment, or both. Indeed, it is precisely the political need to mitigate sectoral consequences of monetary policy that leads to conflicts between the independent Federal Reserve Board, the administration, and the Congress.

There are also occasions when monetary policy overwhelms other economic policies, creating waste and confusion—for example, when tight money limits bank funds to be loaned at a subsidized interest rate to small business under the Small Business Administration programs. The interaction of monetary policy with other macro and micro policies needs intensive analysis.

Trade Policy

Trade policy is not ordinarily considered macro policy because it does not address overall goals of maintaining employment, increasing GNP, and controlling inflation. Yet trade policies affect achievement of macro policy goals very strongly.

Trade policies have both strategic and economic objectives. Simplistically stated, the strategic objectives are to maintain access to materials critical for survival and to forge beneficial alliances with other nations that will be stable over time. The economic objective of trade policy is to promote opportunities for marketing the products of American firms. To do this means that American markets must be reasonably open to foreign goods, because otherwise foreign markets may not be open to American producers. The United States is a cosigner of the General Agreement on Tariffs and Trades (GATT), which for over 25 years has provided a framework for orderly international trade, tariff reduction, elimination of non-tariff trade barriers, and settlement of trade disputes. These and other trade issues must take into account the need of American consumers to have access to products at reasonable prices as well as the need of American workers (who, of course, are also consumers) to have jobs. Although in a particular case certain interest groups may be dissatisfied with a particular trade agreement, in general the GATT has served the United States well.

Both policy toward imports and policy toward exports influence the competitive position of U.S. firms, industries, and sectors. Trade-adjustment assistance, a consequence of import policy, is also relevant because it aims to compensate American firms and workers and communities that are disproportionately disadvantaged by imports permitted under binational and multinational trade agreements.

The main issues regarding trade policy are who benefits and who pays when government artificially protects domestic industry from competition. Clearly, only a few benefit. But these few can be politically powerful. For example, primary sectors, such as steel and aluminum, are protected from foreign competition through both quotas and price mechanisms. This protection or trade screen helps maintain high production costs not only in those sectors but also in other basic durable goods, such as automobiles and aircraft. This in turn diminishes the price competitiveness of American products in those sectors. Trade screens for primary metals thus contribute to Americans' preference for foreign cars and help depress sales of United States-made vehicles.

But counterproductive export policies have also hamstrung U.S. firms. For example, while governments in other countries financed exports, the U.S. Export Import Bank, which helps finance exports of U.S. goods, was leashed by extensive statutory and regulatory limitations, such as that which limited liabilities to ten times capital or the requirement for 10-percent reserves. The Stevenson amendments to the Edge Act in the International Banking Act of 1978 removed most of these restrictions and allowed export organizations (the so-called Edge Act Corporations) greater latitude. The Export-Import Bank's powers were also extended in 1978, and the Bank's annual trek to Capitol Hill was eliminated by extending the Bank's authority for five years and increasing its aggregate commitment authority to $4.1 billion for fiscal year 1980.

Export assistance alone does not guarantee an export market, of course. Other countries must open up to our goods. Japan has the highest barriers against American goods and was the main focus of attention during the 1979 Tokyo round of trade negotiations. Japanese tariffs on U.S. industrial products were reduced about 60 percent, which was particularly welcome in industries producing electronics, scientific instruments, computers, and construction equipment. Although these achievements immediately improved the terms of trade, others must follow if trade is to be competitive. Japanese discretionary import licensing, tax rebates, inflation insurance for exporters, and exemption of income earned from domestically manufactured exports from income taxation all help make U.S. goods too expensive for consumption in Japan while helping Japanese goods to undercut American goods in the United States.

In 1979 the administration reorganized the international trade function to increase the volume of exports, facilitate the enforcement of U.S. trade laws, and implement the agreements achieved during the Tokyo round. The reorganization proposal prepared by the Office of Management and Budget and Robert Strauss, at that time the Special Trade Representative, articulated the need to improve coordination between trade-policy goals and other U.S. policy objectives. No mechanism now exists to accomplish this objective. But the objective is more important now than when it was agreed on. As the United States weathers a period of severe recession, domestic demand will taper off and exports will be more needed to maintain production at capacity. Germany and Switzerland teach us that export-support policy must be supported by restraining domestic purchasing power and controlling imports through fiscal and monetary measures. These policies echo eighteenth-century mercantilism in a twentieth-century context. But the only substitute for totally free trade is limited trade aimed to mutually beneficial national goals of all nations. While working toward a free-trade goal, U.S. policy must recognize reality and act appropriately to the circumstances of a neomercantile world system.

Trade-Adjustment Assistance and Industrial Policy

The United States, alone with Canada among the OECD countries, divorces trade-adjustment assistance from general industrial policies.[1] The Trade Adjustment Act of 1974, the last in the series of measures designed to compensate firms and workers (and communities) damaged by import competition, has never been considered a tool for economic growth but rather a political necessity to meet the demands of organized labor (and to some extent organized business) for protection. The Trade Adjustment Act (TAA) has cushioned the negative impact of lowering trade barriers on industries with large numbers of employees—particularly the apparel, shoe, textile, and steel industries.

By the end of 1979, 179 firms and 467,000 workers had been assisted monetarily. But TAA programs have not been very effective in facilitating structural adjustment by moving workers from low-demand to high-demand industries or sectors or by increasing the efficiency of firms in trade-sensitive operations. Assistance to firms has been only minor, and worker assistance has amounted to little more than supplementary unemployment insurance. The program, even were it not hamstrung by eligibility criteria that cannot reasonably be met, can make little difference to long-run economic performance.

A more acceptable alternative to trade-adjustment assistance is to encourage efficiency in all firms in all communities. Combined with an extensive program of information on export potential, this would increase the worldwide competitive advantage of American firms. The tools of TAA could be applied to firms with a potential for success, not merely to firms (and their workers) on the brink of bankruptcy. They include grants for upgrading capital equipment or, as an alternative, low-interest loans with repayment holidays; and technical assistance to plan for increased productivity, new product design, management innovations, and other procedures, which in additon to upgrading capital equipment will contribute to higher efficiency.

Programs to facilitate worker adjustment to structural economic change must be functional, not merely a handout. They must include occupational training and general assistance in living accommodations if they are to be successful. Ways to encourage occupational mobility are needed. For example, workers might be less reluctant to participate in retraining programs if their fringe benefits were assured.

Industrial policy would also obviate the need for assistance to communities in trade-related economic decline, which has never been funded or implemented under the Trade Adjustment Act. Some analysts have suggested that community assistance would be workable if eligibility were based on a threshold level of import impact. This does not appear to be feasible. For example, a community having 8 percent of its highly paid work force in one industry jobless could legitimately argue that import penetration affected it more severely than a 10-percent job loss among very low paid unskilled workers. In short, community-oriented alleviation of economic hardship is more cumbersome and costly than the alternative: a strategy to encourage efficiency and redeploy workers no longer needed in specific industries or places.

Antitrust Policy

Regulation of corporate size and concentration in the nation's industries is based on legislation almost a century old. The Sherman Antitrust Act was passed in 1890, in a period when uncontrolled speculation had made millionaires of a few while leaving the most vital spurs to national growth in the control of a handful of entrepreneurs. The major modifications to antitrust law, in the Clayton Act of 1914, are also more than a half-century old.

These laws are enforced inconsistently and sporadically. But the conditions that spawned them have completely changed. What was a closed national economy is now an open economy. What was an adolescent economy is now a mature economy. What was a resource-wasting economy is now becoming a resource-conserving economy.

It is time to take a new look not only at how the existing legislation is implemented and enforced but also at the statutes themselves. For some industries that are now fragmented, economies of scale may be the primary requisite to improving competitive position. The paper industry is an example. A multi-billion-dollar industry with steady demand, the industry is constantly plagued by cost pressures, among them the steadily escalating and uncertain costs of pulp. But paper manufacturers are prohibited from forming consortia to bid jointly on pulp purchases, even on a regional basis. Since small-lot purchases are more expensive than large-lot purchases, existing regulations deprive the industry of an opportunity for cost savings.

Another aspect of antitrust law that is of concern is its depressing effect on innovation. One of the more vocal spokesmen for business, Reginald Jones, chairman and chief executive officer of General Electric Company, has noted often that increased market share resulting from new technology is actionable in monopoly cases. Jones' insistence that corporations are discouraged from developing and marketing new products if they are not permitted to profit from the exercise undoubtedly holds some truth.

Antitrust statutes should not inhibit market entry in key industries. Some industries that are now highly concentrated are not producing goods the nation desperately needs to prosper and to improve the quality of life. For example, the public-transportation equipment sector, dominated by fewer than five firms, is not keeping up with the national demand for buses or railway and subway cars. Indeed, the cost of, quality of, and time needed to buy domestic transportation equipment are such that foreign goods are far more attractive to American consumers—mainly local governments or transportation authorities. In this case, government might well move more aggressively to encourage competition, not only through relevant antitrust actions and trade policy but also by encouraging new firms to enter the market and become profitable. More will be said about this later.

Area-Development Policy

Area-development policies include policies aimed at specified geographical areas and policies that, although not confined to a territory defined by statute, chiefly affect the development potential of particular areas. Among them are federal-land policies, mineral and timber policies, and water-supply policies. These and other resource-management policies can significantly affect industrial production.

Distressed-areas policies are designed to bring regions or subregions to a higher level of income and employment. The means to do so include vital-resource management; investment in public works and basic infrastructures—highways, water supply, and sewers; investment in social infrastructure—schools, nurseries, day-care centers, hospitals, and clinics; investment in human resources—job-training programs and vocational counseling; and fiscal incentives to industry to provide jobs in these areas—tax abatement, credits, and exemption from federal taxation of revenue bonds for financing.

Originally, federal economic-development assistance was directed to rural and semirural areas with primary economies—agricultural, timber, or mining bases. Many of these policies were introduced in the 1930s, and in the course of 45 years they successfully set the stage for development in the lagging areas. By the 1960s it had become apparent that economic distress was not confined to the areas of primary economic activity but extended to areas of secondary activity (manufacturing) and even to areas of tertiary activity (service sector) as well. The Area Redevelopment Act of 1961 and its successor, the Public Works and Economic Development ACT (PWEDA) of 1965, responded to this change in circumstances; but they produced a confusion of objectives and measures that still confound development policies today.

PWEDA, though geared to distressed areas of "substantial and persistent unemployment," evades the problem of determining how, in pursuing the goal of increasing jobs in such areas, government is to encourage both production and productivity while also increasing employment. It is possible to raise production and jobs at a very low level of efficiency; it is possible to have a very high level of efficiency without creating many jobs or increasing output; and it is possible to create jobs without achieving gains in efficiency or output.

Legislation creating other spatial policies also confuses end and means. For example, the Rural Development Act of 1972 provided for infrastructure loans and grants to be available to all areas defined as rural—not only those in economic distress. Thus subsidies for economically stable rural areas can be greater than subsidies for distressed urban areas.

Most regional investment has been in physical infrastructure. The rationale was that once these major investments were in place, many private investors would gravitate to the improved area. This would have been likely if development opportunities were limited by development restrictions outside the growth points, as is the case in many European countries. But in the United States, the growth-point principle has been sacrificed to politics. Congressmen and senators always want to bring something home for the voters. Thus the pork barrel is regularly refilled, and to keep it full no options can be closed out. Since a successful, concentrated area-development strategy is precluded without concomitant disincentives in nongrowth areas, the result is sprawl. For example, the Appalachian regional highway system, though intended to strengthen the linkages between designated growth points within the region, actually helped lure industries and firms away from the growth points to be strung along the highways themselves. Inefficiencies resulting from spread-out facilities and diseconomies of scattered, small-scale activity plague many regions.

The main point, however, is that public investment in these regions, though intended to strengthen the economic base of the region, is targeted not to industries but rather to places (or, some insist, to people in places). If one excludes marginal cottage industries for indigenous crafts at one extreme and military-NASA activities at the other extreme, one finds few examples of regional-development investment being tied to private-sector investment or geared to the requirements of particular industries.

The debate over the Public Works and Economic Development Act of 1980 illustrates the disutility of the distressed-area approach in today's complex economy. The House wanted the programs to be available in 90 percent of the country; the Senate favored limiting aid to two-thirds of the nation. Persuasive economic arguments are lacking for either ratio; both of them are too large to justify area classification as "most" distressed. But pragmatic or functional rationales are hard to come by, because economic activity is now so widely diffused over urban, surburban, and rural areas that underdevelopment is no longer the only or the main problem. In congested, old, urbanized areas, *overdevelopment* is a major part of the problem. Area-wide economic hardship often results from senility in particular industries or firms that have failed to modernize and cannot maintain a competitive position in their markets.

Because of their historical evolution, therefore, distressed-area policies have not hit the real issue: how to simultaneously achieve more production and higher productivity. One without the other may provide a short-lived benefit. New enterprises may create jobs in an area, but unless the enterprises can show productivity gains over the long run, they may not remain economically viable. By this test, moreover, many existing economic-development programs are of little use. About 50 percent of firms assisted by Federal Economic Development Administration secured loans have failed to retire their debt within the initial repayment period—a strong clue that the firms aided will not be economically viable.

It is also possible to achieve a high level of efficiency—and, therefore, profits and taxes—without creating many jobs. Many development officials in the past have shied away from helping capital-intensive enterprises that promised little job growth. But jobs in capital-intensive industries pay high wages and may have a high multiplier effect in their attraction for other related industries.

Labor is a generally neglected but increasingly important factor in regional development. The quality of the local labor supply is often cited by businessmen as a reason for locating in a particular area. Although this is often a euphemism for worker indifference to unionization, and docility, the fact remains that it is advantageous for firms to locate where there is a large, readily available pool of labor willing to work for relatively low wages and likely to be relatively reliable. Thus vocational education and manpower training are essential elements of sectoral strategies for regional development. Far more effective efforts are needed in every region of the country to match labor training and skills to the needs of industry and business. Too many horror stories can be told about present job-training efforts; too many trainees are being trained on obsolete machinery for jobs that do not exist.

The economic success of area-development policies must be measured in terms of productivity, jobs, and value added, or gross regional income, if such policies are to be truly economic and not mere social transfers. Development policies should be coordinated with other national economic policies to increase the efficiency of U.S. firms, expand their output, and secure markets. Successful sectoral policies, over time, should reduce the need for adjustment assistance.

During the late 1970s, the country flirted with a new variation of area-specific policy: urban policy. Intended to encourage job generation and economic revitalization in older cities showing fiscal distress due to economic decline, urban policy, like regional policy, fell prey to politics. Urban policy emphasized economic-development efforts because the problem was initially diagnosed as lack of economic growth in cities. But since many cities that are economically strong also have "problems," such as poor people, in them, it became a political necessity to redefine the problem. Very quickly, impoverished neighborhoods in rich cities and "deprived" neighborhoods in wealthy suburbs came under the urban policy umbrella. The law of political dispersion, ever at work, virtually canceled the laudable concept of targeting development assistance to distressed cities. In its place came a compromise—targeting assistance to distressed *people* wherever they might live, so long as it was not in an area that came under the jurisdiction of a rural act.

According to the Congressional Budget Office Economic Index, 46 percent of our major cities and urban counties are severely distressed economically and fiscally. This means that 54 percent are *not* distressed; yet many in this category receive aid under various urban programs. Aid such as grants for community development based on relative—not absolute—poverty is welcomed by most cities, but such intergovernmental aid is inefficient and may be inequitable.

The reason urban policy has been so ineffective is that it begins at the wrong end of the problem. The reason for our durable and intransigent urban economic decline is that industry is not keeping up with world and domestic opportunities. The decline of hundreds of communities in all regions is the direct result of declining performance of U.S. industries.

Retrenchment in the nation's key manufacturing sectors, the automotive sector and the steel sector, has devastated more than 40 cities from New Jersey to California, from Alabama to Michigan. Ford shutdowns alone affected 13 communities, 10 of which are major cities; some 35,000 workers in these cities were laid off in 1979 by Ford. The Chrysler crisis affected 18 cities in 8 states, hitting some 100,000 workers (see table 4-2). Steel-plant shutdowns affected urban communities in California, Ohio, Pennsylvania, West Virginia, New York, Indiana, and Illinois.

Urban distress has been ameliorated by specific programs, such as the Community Development Block Grant, which entitles distressed communities to a federal grant that can be used for a number of purposes, ranging from neighborhood renewal through economic development to social services; Urban Development Action Grants, intended to catalyze private

Table 4–2
Chrysler Auto-Production Employment, May 1979

Metropolitan	Number of Plants	Production Employment	Annual Payroll Millions of Dollars	Chrysler Employment as Percentage of Area Manufacturing Employment
Michigan total	25	53,604	1,565	4.6
Ann Arbor	2	1,276	37	3.2
Detroit	22	51,676	1,509	9.0
Lansing-Lyons	1	652	19	1.5
Indiana total	7	13,708	383	1.9
Indianapolis	2	4,042	113	3.1
Kokomo	2	6,764	189	a
Michigan City	1	295	8	a
New Castle	2	2,607	73	a
Ohio total	6	9,405	245	0.7
Dayton	1	1,926	52	1.8
Fostoria	1	652	18	a
Sandusky	1	344	9	a
Toledo	1	2,389	65	2.7
Twinburg	1	3,748	101	a
Van Wert-Lima	1	347	9	a
Missouri total	2	8,900	235	2.0
St. Louis	2	8,900	235	3.5
Illionois total	1	5,076	137	0.4
Belvidere	1	5,076	137	9.4
Delaware total	1	4,477	108	6.5
Newark	1	4,477	108	7.2
New York total	1	3,679	112	0.2
Syracuse	1	3,679	112	5.5
Alabama total	1	1,741	41	0.5
Huntsville	1	1,741	41	6.7

Source: U.S. Department of Transportation, *Employment and Economic Effects of a Chrysler Shutdown or Major Reduction in Business: Preliminary Data and Analysis* (draft staff study), reported in Peter Trapper and Amy Abrams, "The Regional Impact of the Crisis at Chrysler" (Washington, D.C.: Northeast-Midwest Institute, 1979)

[a] Less than 0.5 percent

investment in commercial construction projects, which will create jobs; the Economic Development Administration programs to help business and industry remain viable; and Trade-Adjustment Assistance to firms and workers in cities whose industrial decline can be nominally attributed to competitive imports. These programs are but a finger in the proverbial dike. Of what use are new sewers or industrial parks in cities if industry is shrinking?

Not only our older, heavily industrial metropolitan areas are in deep trouble, however. Growing cities, too, face uncertainties and probable economic dislocation in the near future. Growing cities generally are based on so-called high-technology industries: energy, electronics, telecommunications, scientific instruments, and high services. But the high-technology industries are not invulnerable to worldwide shifts in production and markets. In most other advanced industrial countries, government and industry are partners in a new push to capture high-technology and service markets on a global scale. For example, Japan, Britain, France, and Germany are chipping away at U.S. sales in the semiconductor industry. They have entered the biochemical sector. They have spent large sums for research and development in scientific instruments and automated control systems. If the United States cannot maintain a strong role in these industries, even the apparently booming economies of the growth areas may soon feel the consequences of declining sales for locally produced goods.

Perhaps what is needed is an urban policy that will better separate the place issues from the people issues, the government issues from the private-sector issues, and the fiscal issues from the economic issues. The solutions to many urban problems do not lie in a community-oriented area-development policy as much as in a new policy to advance America's competitive economic position.

National sectoral policies can lay to rest the perennial dilemma of how to target urban programs. Our traditional programs have created the monster of inequitable political formulas to identify eligible areas and distribute their entitlements to federal aid. Every election year, debate rages as to whether the sunbelt or the frostbelt is being shortchanged by these formulas. At the same time, rural and urban, metropolitan and nonmetropolitan communities vie for what they see as their fair share of federal largesse.

Although the number of places eligible for direct federal assistance has grown, many communities that are far from poor by an absolute national standard have received federal aid. This is possible because comparisons are made on the basis of data that have no relevance to poverty, such as age of housing stock. At the same time, many communities that have not realized their own revenue-generating limits—or, in other words, have a relatively low local tax burden—receive federal aid.

By dealing with the problems of industries and sectors first, and considering their distribution over the landscape only second, the government can encourage economic growth without making artificial and sometimes arbitrary distinctions among eligible places. It is far more efficient to use federal tax dollars to breathe new life into existing economic endeavors than to try to create from scratch businesses and industries where they do not now exist. To be sure, there will be communities that were relatively well off in the past that become eligible for federal aid under industry-specific guidelines; and some federal aid might be diverted from communities that have a long history of impoverishment. The trade-off is that the former have a realistic chance of rebuilding their economies, while the latter have a much smaller chance.

Existing Sectoral Policies

Among the policies that have a bearing on the economic potential of the United States are those that are now labeled "sectoral." Sectoral policies for mining, agriculture, the maritime industry, fisheries, and housing now exist. Regulation of these sectors or incentives to encourage production in them can have positive impacts on the manufacturing and service sectors. For example, cheaper agricultural by-products can lower costs of consumer and durable goods that use them as inputs. Mineral policy affects manufacturing, because the pace at which mineral resources are developed and stockpiled affects the costs of manufacturing firms in many industries. Availability and expected availability of basic minerals influence capital-investment decisions in industries dependent on them as inputs, which in turn influences the productivity of American firms and their competitive advantage in world markets. Countless examples of such interrelationships could be offered.

Another type of micro policy, which is incorrectly labeled "sectoral," is small-business policy. Federally guaranteed loans are available to small business as a class. Together with technical assistance, these low-cost loans, supplied through the Small Business Administration, are intended to relieve the credit problems faced by small firms even in the best of financial times. Firms with limited net worth cannot easily secure well-priced mortgage financing, financing for new equipment, venture capital, or working capital. A small firm often must pay higher rates for capital than larger firms. During credit-tight periods, small firms are even more disadvantaged and are the first to feel the impact of tight money policies.

In addition to the Small Business Administration program, a $1.8 billion business-development program, aimed at small and medium-sized firms and to be administered by the Economic Development Administration

(EDA) in the Department of Commerce, is pending in 1980. Direct loans, loan guarantees, and interest subsidies would be financed by the federal government on terms that ignore the type of industry of which an applicant firm is a part.

Complicated and perhaps impossible judgments are required to administer a program aimed at size-categories of firms. They are mythical beasts—the "small" business may be a one-man candy store or a thousand-person assembly-line operation. The Small Business Administration recently raised the limits defining eligibility for financial assistance. Although it was intended to adjust for inflation, the rule change implicitly recognized that size is relative; a firm that is big in one industry may be small in another; and the economic value of a given subsidy may be greater for a slightly larger firm than for a small one. At present, the economic pay-off of the small-business program is hardly considered. The Small Business Administration judges program success solely on the basis of which companies default on their loans and which do not. It seldom knows whether an assisted firm has become more stable, has expanded employment, has expanded output, or has increased its profits. Thus neither the Small Business Administration nor Congress is in a position to know whether or not the program contributes to the productivity of the country. These problems would be avoided if the credit assistance were directed to key industries determined to be valuable to the American economy.

Regulatory Interventions

In the past two decades, government regulation of business and industry has mushroomed. Virtually every type of private-sector economic decision is affected by government standards. In 1979 the federal government printed more than 75,000 pages of regulatory guidelines. These guidelines are administered by a plethora of agencies. Depending on whether White House or General Accounting Office estimates are accepted, there are either 90 or 116 federal regulatory agencies, some a formal part of the Executive Branch and others independent.

Regulation directly affects rates and tariffs, conditions of competition, conditions for market entry and exit, product-performance standards, workplace conditions, and environmental consequences of economic activity. To enforce regulations, much reporting and disclosure is required of firms. Firms must be prepared to meet or comply with precise objectives. Often the terms and conditions under which they must be achieved are also specified.

Despite the large number of agencies involved in regulatory activity and the thousands of pages of rules to be enforced, the government pays less to regulate business than business pays to be regulated. For example, in fiscal year 1978 the direct costs to the nation's businesses for installation of pollution-control and abatement equipment was over $22 billion.[2] However, the direct administration and monitoring costs to the federal government were only $829 million—about 3.8 percent of the direct business expenditures. In testimony to the Congress in 1978, former Secretary of Commerce Juanita Kreps estimated regulatory costs to firms in the range of $60 billion to $130 billion annually.[3] The Federal Commission on Paperwork estimated the compliance paperwork required from private-sector firms to be in the range of $25 billion to $32 billion in 1977.[4] Of this amount, approximately $18 billion was directly attributable to regulatory requirements.

The substantial direct and hidden costs to business are reflected in lower gross national product and higher production costs in specific industries and for individual firms. In practice, government regulation imposes a hidden tax on economic activity. The nature and consequences of this hidden tax are not fully understood. In some sectors, such as the transportation sector, reduction or elimination of government regulation has taken place only during the last two years, and other events, such as the huge rise in fuel prices, have obscured the outcomes of deregulation. However, it is essential to examine the effects of regulation on key industries and sectors and to determine the costs to business and benefits to society of alternatives.

A particular concern should be the effect of regulation on innovation. Meeting compliance, documentation, and time costs imposed by regulatory bodies is often so difficult that it inhibits production of new products. For example, present regulations to ensure drug safety impose a four-year delay before new drugs can be marketed. This means that new-drug development and refinement tends to be more financially feasible for the largest firms, which can afford to wait it out and defer profits. It also means that pharmaceutical firms are encouraged to produce more of those drug improvements that will have the widest markets and profit potential and less of the limited-use drugs that may be critical for relatively small numbers of patients. Although no one would advocate irresponsibly speeding up the pharmaceutical-testing timetable, a flexible schedule based on technical standards rather than arbitrary operational rules would be advisable.

The main point here is that regulations must be administered so as to take into consideration the costs imposed by them on business and their ultimate impact on production levels, types of goods and services available, and contribution to efficiency.

An example of this approach is a 1979 analysis by the Department of Commerce of the cumulative effects of regulatory actions on the copper industry.[5] The projected impact of a select set of regulations was assessed in terms of capacity and production restraints, the costs of compliance to the industry, and the economic consequences to the nation. The analysis concluded that full compliance by the copper industry with existing air, water, worker-health, and land-use legislation in the period 1970–1979 would have resulted in

1. Probable shutdown of three major smelters and decrease in domestic refined-copper capacity by 3 percent;
2. An increase in net imports of copper from a previously projected 11 percent to 15 percent of domestic copper consumption;
3. Loss of a projected 31,000 new jobs;
4. The need for an additional investment of $1.8 billion of capital costs and $1.7 billion of operating costs that would not be made otherwise— even as capacity was reduced by 3 percent;
5. An increase in copper prices 43 percent greater than would normally be expected—thus feeding inflation and destroying much of the nation's comparative advantage in copper production.

The problems associated with implementation of regulatory policy are the problems of any adolescent system. Legitimate national goals couched in obscure legislative language require trial and error before efficient implementation systems can be devised, promulgated, and enforced. The major point being made here is that while the difficulties of the regulatory system itself have come to be rather widely recognized, few have recognized the interdependence of the regulatory system with other economic policies. These interdependencies must be made visible and comprehensible. A system for cross-referencing regulatory-policy implementation with macro and micro policy objectives should be established.

The Costs of Delay

Partly as a result of increasingly complex government regulations, but also the result of private-sector mismanagement, simple delay is costing the country a fortune. Construction delays are the most easily measured. The construction sector is an exceedingly complex chain: it involves landowners, lenders, developers, and suppliers of finished construction materials; suppliers of wood, steel, concrete, aluminum, and plastic; suppliers of finish materials, such as hardware; contractors and subcontractors; suppliers and manufacturers of cranes, bulldozers, and other heavy equipment; several crafts unions; and local, state, and federal governments. Rather than becoming more efficient with modern technology, the construction industry is notoriously inefficient. Capital investment has not increased productivity in the industry; according to the American Productivity Center, productivity has declined since 1965.[6] If we go back even further, it is shocking that the relatively unsophisticated construction sector of 1931 completed the Empire State Building in less than 14 months from ground-breaking and now construction of the new Philip Hart Senate Office Building will require at least ten years. In the 1960s it took less than five years to build a new electric power plant. Now, it takes more than ten years. As a result, approximately $40 billion of the nation's $122 billion public-utility budget is financing delay.[7]

This slowdown means that much public and private expenditure finances delay by stretching out interest payments, inflating payroll costs for underutilized personnel, and eroding purchasing power through inflation. The U.S. economy is now losing an estimated $10 billion per year in purchasing power by construction delay in public works alone.

Delay in the public sector obviously eats away the benefits of public programs. The Department of Housing and Urban Development is losing almost $600 million of purchasing power annually because it has a $3 billion backlog in capital projects funded by its Community Development Block Grant program. The Economic Development Administration entered fiscal year 1980 with a 10-percent backlog in its funds that were "fast-tracked" in 1976–1977 to combat joblessness induced by the 1974–1975 recession. This backlog totaled 10 percent of the $6 billion "accelerated" public-works program. In June 1980 the Environmental Protection Agency had an undisbursed backlog of almost $9 billion for community water and sewer projects, some approved as long ago as 1970 but not yet built. The public-works pipeline has a backlog estimated at over $100 billion—two and one-half years' worth of public-works appropriations for all levels of government.

Not all the responsibility for delay in government-funded construction lies with the federal government. Many communities move at a snail's pace when it comes to spending money. As of January 1980, New York City, Los Angeles, and Chicago had spent only 54 percent of their total available Community Development Block Grant funds.

The economic consequences of construction delay ripple through the economy. Obviously, jobs are affected. Construction unemployment in 1980 was estimated at 17 percent nationally and reached 40 percent in many localities. It is evident that, if expenditures were to catch up with intent, hundreds of thousands of construction jobs would quickly be created. In turn, accelelated construction would boost demand for construction materials and equipment, helping prevent job losses in the steel industry and other basic industries.

Delay has political consequences, too. Obviously, Congress will be less enthusiastic about enacting public-works programs, especially accelerated or so-called countercyclical programs, if the programs don't begin to meet the objectives. One study has shown that by the time countercyclical expen-

ditures are made, the country is out of recession and into rampant inflation, so that these programs contribute to more sudden and precipitous
cyclical changes in the economy, rather than merely evening out the business cycle.[8]

Delay-generated costs also have a depressing effect on quality-of-life
programs, such as environmental protection, worker health and safety, and
consumer protection. There is a great deal of political pressure to postpone
or cut back these programs, whose high cost to business and industry is
cited as a major contributor to low productivity. Savings from reduced
construction delays could easily offset the costs of compliance with these
regulations. For example, the value of environmental-protection investments of both the public and private sectors in 1979 was $42 billion—
roughly equal to the delay costs in public-utility construction.[9]

Eliminating the high cost of delay is not a simple task, because so many
individuals and agencies are involved. It is a management task that can be
carried out, however, as the national effort to place an American on the
moon proved in the early 1960s. It involves, first, accurate estimates of the
costs of delay; second, an accounting procedure that includes these costs as
debits against all program budgets; third, a mechanism for eliminating the
choice of inaction; fourth, a mechanism for tracking projects regularly; and
fifth, an incentive system that rewards construction managers for beating
the deadlines, rather than postponing them. These management changes
will be discussed further in chapter 5.

Notes

1. Ironically, it is the very existence of comprehensive industrial policies in other countries, including government procurement practices, selec-
tive subsidies on exports and production, regional development policies,
subsidized public services, and adjustment assistance that led to the inser-
tion of Section 102 into the Trade Act of 1974. Section 102 pinpointed the
pervasiveness of nontariff trade barriers and called for the U.S. negotiators
to eliminate or minimize them; this became the objective of the Tokyo
round of negotiations in the summer of 1979.

2. U.S., Department of Commerce, Bureau of Economic Analysis,
Survey of Current Business, vol. 59, no. 2 (Washington, D.C.: U.S. Government Printing Office, February 1979), p. S-32.

3. U.S., Congress, Joint Economic Committee, *The Cost of Government Regulation* (Washington, D.C.: U.S. Government Printing Office,
April 1978), p. 5.

4. See Timothy D. Mead, *The Impact of Federal Paperwork on State*

and Local Government (Columbus, Ohio: Academy for Contemporary Problems, 1977) for a full discussion of the paperwork problem.

5. U.S., Department of Commerce, *The Potential Economic Impact of U.S. Regulations on the U.S. Copper Industry* (Washington, D.C.: U.S. Government Printing Office, April 1979), p. I-1-3.

6. Total factor productivity declined at an average annual rate of 2 percent in the 1965–1973 period and 1.3 percent in the 1973–1978 period. Carolyn A. Meanley, ed., *Productivity Perspectives* (Houston: American Productivity Institute, 1980) p. 7.

7. The estimates were first compiled by Pat Choate for *As Time Goes By: The Costs and Consequences of Delay* (Columbus, Ohio, and Washington, D.C.: Academy for Contemporary Problems, 1980).

8. Georges Vernez and Roger Vaughan, *Assessment of Countercyclical Public Works and Public Service Employment Programs* (Santa Monica: Rand Corporation, 1978).

9. *Survey of Current Business,* February 1979, p. 15.

5 Anatomy of Sectoral Policies

Development-oriented sectoral policies must be articulated in the context of macroeconomic goals of reducing inflation and achieving full employment. They must be harmonized with the goals of balanced national growth and economic development. They must be pursued within the framework of national budget-management objectives and international concerns.

Sectoral policies have been successful on a smaller scale than that needed for major sectors, such as the automotive sector. For example, as a result of improvements in domestic productivity resulting from increased capital investment, combined with successful negotiations to create an orderly international textile market, the U.S. textile sector significantly increased its excess of exports over imports in 1979. This occurred even though imports were not reduced. The textile sector was reaping the reward of deliberate efforts to specialize in goods that can be produced at low per-unit costs by new equipment, including lasers, computers, and jet-air looms. These goods—such as drapes and upholstery materials—and the raw materials to make them were marketable to countries that either lacked the domestic capacity to weave them at all or could not compete on a price-quality basis with the capital-intensive American product. The textile success story was boosted in earlier stages by some protection from imports. It might well serve as a model for sectoral policies.

The criteria for selecting sectors should be growth potential and adjustment need. The former should be the larger category, and would include all those manufacturing and service operations that promise high employment, high value added, including income and taxes, relative long-term stability, or growth. The other category would include the sectors now aided by trade-adjustment assistance. Where efficiency and productivity are low and cannot be improved, long-term subsidies may well be unjustified. Then the concern is to cushion shock for workers and make the phase-out period as efficient and painless as possible, given the relative costs involved in maintaining unprofitable operations or supporting unemployed workers.

The basic question with regard to assistance to any given firm is whether a government subsidy today will create the conditions under which the assisted firm will become competitive tomorrow. If it does not do so within a given time, either the assistance must be discontinued or the operation must be made a direct public responsibility. Otherwise, taxpayers' money is subsidizing shareholders, entrepreneurs, and bankers to no public benefit. Making this decision on an industry-by-industry basis gives policy analysts, legislators, and administrators a context in which to place the record of each firm's performance. But this kind of evaluation cannot be done by individuals unfamiliar with the cost structure, labor-market conditions, financing options, and international trade opportunities in a given industry. And while there may be exceptions to the profitability rule whereby a permanent subsidy to firms or industries is desirable on social grounds, an economic assessment is still necessary to determine the true cost to the government of continuing the subsidy and to estimate the difference between costs and benefits.

Industry-specific policies should absorb some policies now in effect. Legislation will be needed to remove existing barriers to modernization and upgrading of production and management systems. Among the options are research and development grants, grants or loans for computerization and automation, grants for management training, and credits for retiring obsolete or semiobsolete equipment and moving into a new generation before the previous generation is fully amortized. These supports should be offered not on a worst-first or across-the-board basis but on an industry-wide or sectorwide basis. The public good will be served, because as firms' timetables for innovation advance, they will become more profitable, pay higher income taxes, and be in a position to improve wages and benefits without cutting into profits or limiting their borrowing capacity.

Keeping Ford, etc., in Our Future

Since the near-bankruptcy of the Chrysler Corporation in the fall of 1979, a growing consensus has emerged on the need for federal aid to the automotive sector. The automotive sector is the sector of greatest concern to elected officials because automobile manufacture has historically been the largest source of manufacturing employment. "What's good for General Motors is good for the U.S.A." was a slogan expressing a fundamental economic reality. The automotive sector contributed an estimated $82 billion to the gross national product in 1979.[1] While the actual assembly of automobiles contributed 22 percent to this total, additional economic activity was created in dependent industries: machine tools, tires, rubber, batteries, aluminum, steel, upholstery, plastics, petroleum, and, more recently, electronics (see figure 5-1).

With American auto production down 23 percent in the first half of 1980 and more than 245,000 auto workers laid off, the inroads of foreign producers in American markets were spectacular. Imports, which accounted for slightly over 15 percent of domestic sales in 1970, will account for almost 30 percent of domestic sales in 1980.[2]

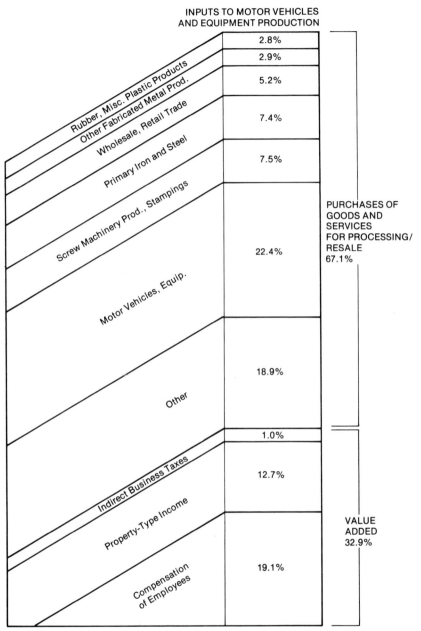

INPUTS TO MOTOR VEHICLES
AND EQUIPMENT PRODUCTION

EQUALS 100% OF INDUSTRY OUTPUT

Source: *1980 U.S. Industrial Outlook* (Washington, D.C.: U.S. Department of Commerce, 1980).

Figure 5–1. Distribution of Inputs, Motor Vehicles and Equipment-
Manufacturing Industries

Proposed remedial policies include fencing off the foreigners, either permanently or temporarily, with tariffs or quotas; tax credits for retooling to produce smaller, more fuel-efficient vehicles; tax write-offs, grants, or loans for pollution-control equipment; and increased benefits for laid-off workers through trade-adjustment assistance or other supplementary income.

The problem with these proposals is that they have not been advanced in a consensus forum. Rather, each interested party—various government agencies, the United Automobile Workers, and the corporations whose leaders have held differing views on what is needed—has presented its alternatives directly to the public in a politically charged atmosphere. This is not the way a sectoral strategy should be crafted. Complex, purposeful negotiations among all affected groups are needed. These negotiations must lead to commitments by each party. The objectives must be to attain higher capital and labor productivity in as short a time as possible and to increase market share by providing better-quality products at competitive prices. If temporary subsidies are required from the government to permit this, they must be granted in exchange for contingent agreements by labor and management to take action. Labor may have to accept a temporary reduction in real earnings. Management may have to make financial sacrifices and give up some heretofore exclusive prerogatives to schedule and order the work. What is certain is that a sectoral strategy must be tripartite if it is to have any chance of success.

To arrive at such a strategy, all parties need a much more specific understanding of existing and potential microeconomic forces. Targets for production must be established, by location and by plant. The amount of capital needed and the time frame within which it is needed must be estimated realistically. Contingency plans should the capital not be forthcoming must be agreed on.

All of this will not be easy. What is different now from any previous moment in history is that, for the first time it is feasible. One year ago, the notion that sectoral policies are practicable and desirable was greeted as heretical and antithetical to the traditions of "a free" economy. Now it is clear that sectoral policies, which offer *every* competitor within a given sector the same opportunities and the same advantages, are more appropriate to those traditions than the firm-specific assistance of the past. Moreover, the Chrysler "bail-out," by which the federal government guaranteed loans to the corporation despite widespread conviction that the measures would not save the company from bankruptcy, demonstrated that cooperation between industry and government is possible, even though in this instance the cooperation fell far short of what was needed.

A long-term automotive-sector strategy must begin with the structural realities of the international market. The facts are as follows. On the supply side, strong foreign competitors are not going to disappear; they will undoubtedly be strengthened by government support if competition becomes keener. On the demand side, foreign markets will grow more rapidly than the U.S. market, especially after 1985, when the present bulge in the number of young people forming new households diminishes. Domestic sales are expected to grow only 1 to 2 percent annually, as compared to 3 percent in the mid-1970s. Moreover, the nature of domestic demand has shifted permanently to lightweight, fuel-efficient cars. In 1980 it cost an estimated $3,000 per year to drive a 1977 Chevrolet Impala 15,000 miles, the average distance traveled annually by a one-car family of middle income. This means that 20 percent of the family's gross income was eaten up by automobile operating costs. There will still be a call for luxury in the American auto market, but it will be luxury consistent with efficiency and low operating costs.

Recognition of world market forces has already pushed U.S. car manufacturers to rethink and reorganize their production goals. Ford and General Motors have advanced the design of a "world car," a standardized vehicle whose parts can be produced anywhere in the world, assembled anywhere in the world, and sold to growing markets in developing countries. The world car permits corporations to achieve economies of scale in markets otherwise too small to support them. Many more parts are interchangeable. Many more activities can be standardized. The more undifferentiated a product, the more easily it can be produced by low-skilled labor. Quality control can be automated. This allows dispersal of production to many sites in low-wage locations close to markets, or even distant from markets when labor costs are low enough to offset the costs of transporting cars to the markets.

By giving up its past style-dominated approach to markets, the American automobile industry has belatedly entered a new era of competition. Whether the planned U.S. products can match the success of the first mass-market car, the Ford Model T, or the minimal cars of the past, such as the Volkswagen Beetle, the two-cylinder Citroen Deux Chevaux, or the Fiat Toppolino, in capturing the hearts of economy-conscious customers remains to be seen. However, the new decentralized production system, combined with automation to increase units per worker in domestic assembly plants, will ultimately reduce the number of jobs available in the domestic automotive sector. Although it can be anticipated that high-skill, high-technology tasks, such as designing and engineering, will still be performed by American workers, the number of such jobs may well diminish. Once a design is perfected, it is likely to remain in production with only minor changes. Design engineering will go into efficiency, not fins or headlights. Even engine components may be interchangeable, self-contained units, many of which will be electronically monitored, so that an owner can snap in a new element when old ones fail. (Of course, subsidiary industries providing the frills as consumer items may spring up in some markets, but they will be ancillary, not primary, elements of the sector.)

The main point is that we must be sure that hastily contrived policies to help the automobile industry as it is presently constituted are not in the long run counterproductive. There is no stopping the internationalization of auto production. If American firms do not participate, Japanese, German, Italian, Swedish, and French firms will have the markets all to themselves. Our national objective cannot be to keep all domestic-market auto production in the United States. This would be inflationary and would encourage retaliation against United States-made goods abroad. Our objective *can* be to reap the benefits of world-scale production in the form of repatriated profits. At the same time, domestic producers can be helped to retool as fast as possible. Rebuilding the automotive sector will provide an immediate shot in the arm for its many component industries, such as the machine-tool industry and the tire industry. The process can double the demand for machine-tool makers in the next three years. According to the executive vice president of the National Tooling and Machining Association, 20 million additional man hours will be needed by 1982.[3]

But this industry is cyclical, and the boom won't last. After 1985 the spurt will abate, and it is necessary to anticipate and prepare for shifts in demand for machine-tool output. This highlights the acute need for broad restructuring throughout the entire automotive sector. Other uses for excess U.S. labor, plant, and technology can be found. It is in the national interest to put our auto-manufacturing know-how to new uses. For example, the nation needs many thousands of buses to meet the needs of a modern public-transportation system in an energy-conserving era. But we are importing buses from Canada, Japan, Germany, and even Britain. Until now, the economic incentives for U.S. firms to produce high-quality, price-competitive buses have not overcome the disincentives; in economic terms, need has not been translated into effective demand for the product. Many reasons can be cited for this situation, including government regulations that are inconsistent, uncertain, and conducive to cost escalation; slow payment by local government purchasers; an uneven stream of orders; and disputes over poor product performance, which purchasers blame on manufacturers and manufacturers blame on poor maintenance by purchasers. Government can and should facilitate the domestic production of these much-needed vehicles. Among the options to be considered are government guarantees for loans to finance start-ups of new firms or offshoots of existing corporations; government assurance of a steady stream of purchases extending far enough into the future to warrant the needed investment; and negotiation of disputes, possibly with resolution by an independent arbiter. Government subsidy for manufacture of public-transportation vehicles, which could employ excess auto workers, would certainly be in the national interest and might even be politically more feasible than subsidies for production of personal-transportation vehicles.

Experiments in Sectoral Policy: The Steel Tripartite Advisory Committee

A joint business-labor-government effort to deal with structural problems in the steel industry has been under way since 1977. A presidential task force on steel (the Solomon Task Force) recommended, among other things, that a Steel Tripartite Advisory Committee undertake not only specific actions to cushion the shock of steel-plant closings on workers and communities but also long-range evaluations of conditions affecting the industry's performance and output. The Committee established five working groups to deal with capital formation, international trade, environmental regulation, technology, and labor issues.

The June 1980 reports of the working groups indicated that their effort had been limited primarily to reviewing existing documentation of the problems facing steel companies. Although the reports reflected a sense of snowballing crisis—fed, no doubt, by the 1980 bankruptcy declaration of Wisconsin Steel, which in 1979 received massive infusions of government loans from the Economic Development Administration—they failed both to relate the issues of concern to one another and to define an integrated plan of action to deal with them.

The Working Group on Modernization and Capital Formation, which includes three members of the government (representing three different federal agencies), four representatives of the steel industry (representing four different companies), and two representatives of labor, concluded that a major capital shortage faces the industry. It quantified this shortage at $1 billion to $1.2 billion per year, basing the figure on the assumption that the steel industry would operate at 90 percent of capacity—a highly unrealistic premise. The steel industry has operated at that high level only in war time and in unusual periods, such as 1972–1973. It is now operating at less than 55 percent of capacity.[4]

Where the report on capital formation falls completely short, in the policy sense, is in its failure to explain the reasons for the projected capital shortage and to assess the effect that various policy changes might have on it. Although the report projects a healthy return on investment in the steel industry, it does not indicate whether an even higher return could help close the capital gap. It leaves unexplored the crucial question of the impact of proposed accelerated depreciation for plant, equipment, and vehicles on the industry's access to capital. It is equally silent on the potential impact of proposed new-investment tax credits or the effect on capital formation of specific programs now in effect, such as Economic Development Administration financial backing for new facilities producing steel rail. In short, it is a largely uncritical review and endorsement of data initially prepared by the American Iron and Steel Institute and, as such, can hardly be considered a viable information base for policy purposes.

The Working Group on Technology, Research and Development, whose findings should presumably influence the conclusions of the Modernization and Capital Formation Group, inventoried technologies and attempted to assess the rate of their incorporation into operating plants. Comparing domestic technological advance with that of Japanese and European steel companies, the group concluded that the United States is lagging behind. That information has been readily available and well publicized since 1975. Astoundingly, the group report concludes that the industry itself is not to be faulted for failing to adopt new techniques; this was merely the result of lack of capital. The report does not attempt to explain why the industry failed to attract sufficient capital.

The Working Group on Community and Labor Adjustment Assistance, which was concerned with concrete actions, listed a number of efforts to get benefits to laid-off workers faster. It recommended that the vehicle for doing so, the Commerce-Labor Adjustment Action Committee, be called to respond to any future plant closings, noting, however, that its success had so far been slight, since it had not gone into action until months after the plants had closed. The report noted that in the future it might be more effective if the "action group" had 90 days' advance notice (as now required by union contracts) before a proposed shutdown. But it made no specific recommendations as to what should be done, given such limited notice, nor did it claim that the committee had authority to take advance action.

The report of the Environmental Protection Subcommittee revealed limited progress in reducing for the steel industry unnecessary costs of compliance with air- and water-pollution regulations. It described the process by which the Environmental Protection Administration (EPA) adjusts its enforcement of regulations to the needs of economically unstable industries. Steel plants constitute about one-third of the plants falling in the special category "threatened industries." On the basis of a review of a firm's balance sheet, the EPA and the firm negotiate compliance schedules, penalties for noncompliance, and levels of required compliance. It is difficult to understand how this could be a cost-effective process. Given the legal and auditing costs, plus the costs of negotiation, an outright grant or subsidized loan to the firm for immediate compliance might well cost the taxpayers far less than this tedious, case-by-case process. The public interest in improved environmental quality would certainly be better served.

None of the Steel Tripartite Advisory Committee working groups can produce a useful contribution to a national steel policy in the circumstances under which they now operate. The groups have no mandate to go beyond the superficial. They have no instructions to coordinate their activities. They have no policy framework within which to coordinate them. In large measure, the government's primary motive in creating and staffing the advisory committee is an immediate, political one: to get unemployment relief to workers as quickly as possible. At the same time, the advisory committee appears interested in international public relations, satisfying our European allies, who are concerned with the demise of steel sectors in Europe and the United States, that the American government is willing to address this problem. Since the working groups have in fact seldom met, and since all the groups have met together only twice in this critical year for the steel industry, it is clear that form is a substitute for substance.

To devise a true tripartite strategy for the steel industry, the same kind of analysis is needed as is necessary for the automotive sector. First, the domestic and international markets for different types of steel products must be assessed. Second, the capacity of the domestic steel sector to meet effective demand must be evaluated, its production costs estimated, and its production schedules determined. Third, the efforts of other governments to support steel production and export must be identified and quantified. Fourth, the actions needed by government, labor, and business to improve the capability of U.S. steel producers to meet the competition, in specific product lines, at specific relative prices, within a specified time, must be detailed. The cost of making needed changes in each plant must be determined. The return on investment necessary to attract the needed capital to the sector must be evaluated, not by the industry alone, but by the investment community. Only then can measures to close any capital gap be properly evaluated in terms not only of their impact on the steel industry but also of their impact on capital formation in other competing industries.

The federal government is the agency to initiate efforts to devise sectoral policies, and the federal government must take responsibility for coordinating the effort. But many private-sector specialists will also be needed, and they must be drawn not only from the affected industries but from among security analysts, attorneys, and venture capitalists. Both generalists, to relate the specific concerns to overall policy, and specialists will have roles to play in the design and implementation of sectoral strategies.

The following discussion highlights the key requirements, inside and outside the government, for policy for any specific sector. It places particular emphasis on the changes in policy process and management that are needed within the federal government. They include revisions in policymaking machinery, information requirements, and administrative requirements. The recommendations are not exhaustive. They are intended to stimulate the thinking of all parties, in an out of government, having a direct interest in rebuilding the U.S. economy.

The Policymaking Process

The economic policymaking machinery of the federal government is dispersed among more than 30 separate departments and agencies outside the Executive Office of the President. Since 1948, 28 formal presidential, cabinet-level or congressional studies of the federal economic policymaking machinery have been undertaken. Although these efforts have resulted in some improvements, the machinery and processes are still inadequate. Thus we are faced with the need for a twenty-ninth analysis. In the meantime, a number of interim actions can be taken to provide a firm foundation for broader future changes.

Although policy is established by Congress on the initiative either of the legislature or of the incumbent administration, policy success depends on the rules and regulations established by the administration and on the internal procedures of the responsible agencies. Program successes and failures must be reported back through the agencies to their appointed chiefs, to the president, and to Congress so that policy modifications to meet new or redefined goals may be established. Thus, while the main focus of the following discussion is on requirements for changes in policymaking machinery, some vital first-step administrative reforms are also indicated. A holistic approach to future public economic interventions will need:

1. A policymaking machinery that identifies all pertinent decisionmaking agents within Executive Departments and Agencies, the Congress, and the private sector; and a policymaking process that elicits substantive input from each of these identified decisionmakers, on a continuing and regular basis.
2. An analytical capacity for predicting and assessing changing economic circumstances and estimating the direct and indirect consequences of alternative public actions.
3. An administrative machinery that can successfully coordinate policies and programs administered by different agencies.
4. An evaluation system to assist in making policy adjustments.

Time Frame

Public policy must consider both the long and the short term. Policymakers tend to take a short-term view of economic events, and, as a result, economic policy tends toward adjustments to prevent or alleviate hardship.

The time frame of elected officials is the budget process of two years and the business cycle of three to seven years. In political reality their time frame is often as short as a few months.

This limited time horizon often leads to counterproductive policies. To the extent that the business cycle represents balancing occurrences, interventions can disrupt or delay a necessary function. Precipitous short-term incentives or brakes can cause more problems than they solve: for example, tight money pushes credit out of some sectors—notably, housing—and away from small firms, which may have unwanted repercussions in electronics, tool making, and other important industries characterized by many small enterprises. Countercyclical investment incentives have only limited countercyclical outcomes: public works generally do not get under way until the business cycle turns up again; and in the private sector, too, the long lead times for investment decisions suggest that little investment that would otherwise not have taken place is actually induced by countercyclical tax credits and other investment incentives.

If the business-cycle time frame is too short for some policies, however, it is not too short for others. Short-term interventions that are related closely to the characteristics of the cycle include direct job-creation in private industry, through mechanisms such as employee wage subsidies, retraining programs or employee maintenance subsidies to cope with unemployment induced by excess inventory. Government-guaranteed low-cost working-capital loans may be appropriate to allow firms to increase inventory or finance it during tight money periods when build-up is needed. Regulatory policies can influence the short-term performance of firms in certain industries.

Secular shifts, which have more permanent effects on economic well being, demand a different policy time frame. Although "long waves" of 50 years or more may best describe the dominant secular cycle in capitalistic systems, such a long time frame is inappropriate to policymaking. Policymakers can, however, consider an intermediate time frame. Economists have defined intermediary cycles of ten years and 15 to 25 years. Intermediary cycles relate to demand for capital equipment, which in turn depends on the rate at which innovation is incorporated into the production system, the availability of finance, the obsolescence of existing plant and equipment, and public policy objectives. This time horizon is appropriate for development-oriented economic policy, which aims to optimize the utilization of productive factors over the long rather than the short run.

Intermediate-term economic goals and objectives should go beyond th five-year national goals established by the Humphrey-Hawkins Act of 1978. To the act's mandate for setting targets for price stability, levels of gross national product, and employment/unemployment levels should be added specific sectoral objectives. This would provide a framework for program administration and for programming beyond the normal two-year horizon of the budgetary process, within the time necessary to anticipate and prepare for structural economic change. The annual executive-branch report on economic policy objectives and achievements required by the Humphrey-Hawkins Act is a useful policy vehicle. Many components of such a plan are nonpartisan in nature and lend themselves to programming beyond the lifetime of a given administration or Congress.

Stronger Policy Links

Stronger linkages between Congress and the Executive Branch are required to deal with the complexities of sectoral policies. In addition to the opportunities offered by the Humphrey-Hawkins Act, other mechanisms can facilitate communication and interaction to refine policy analysis. The Economic Report of the President, and the president's biannual Urban Policy Report contain elements germane to an integrated economic policy. Congress and the Executive Office might consider whether reporting requirements should be modified to incorporate anticipatory evaluation of the effects on key sectors of fiscal, monetary, area, trade, and regulatory policy goals. It would seem that a coherent and useful report should look ahead to where we want to be, as well as explain why the nation is or is not where it expected to be.

Consultative System within Government

A more extensive and more regular consultative system within the federal government is needed to improve the scope and coherence of economic-policy formulation. Participants in this system must be the presidentially appointed officials with responsibility for implementing policy. They must meet regularly with one another, with the president and his staff, with the Council of Economic Advisors, and with the committee chiefs of the relevant House and Senate committees. A parallel consultative system must be created at the staff level.

A particular effort should be made to bring the Federal Reserve Board, the Federal Home Loan Bank Board, and other politically independent agencies into the consultative system. The Federal Reserve Board is the lead agency in the economic-policy formulation process. Since the turnaround time for monetary policy shifts is much shorter than the turnaround time for fiscal policy and micro policy shifts, early communication, consistent with the Fed's independence, could preclude unwanted or anticipated sectoral dislocations resulting from its decisions.

Improved consultation with representatives of state, county, and municipal government will also be necessary to a more effective policy-formulation process. Many state and local governments have assumed major roles in influencing the nature and direction of subnational development. State and local government intervention in the activities and location choices of firms is growing fast. Subnational governments are particularly concerned with the geographic distribution of problems and opportunities occasioned by federal government policy. They often are the best source of information on the possible consequences of alternative federal, state, or local actions, and could be leaders in an early-warning system for industry-specific problems.

Federal Regulatory Council

The scope, authority, and analytical capacity of the Federal Regulatory Council should be expanded. The creation of the Federal Regulatory Council in 1979 was a major step forward in identifying the breadth of regulatory activities and some of their consequences. The council's members represent 35 regulatory agencies. The council is a communications system for these agencies. This council's limited analytical capacity should be expanded to permit consideration of trade-offs among the respective regulatory activities and among other macro, micro, and sectoral goals. Among the questions the council should explore with Congress is authority to suspend regulatory actions that are inconsistent with national development goals and objectives.

Consultative System in the Private Sector

Sectoral policies aim to remove the barriers to expanded markets, increased profitability, and greater efficiency of American firms. To take appropriate action, government needs a regular system of information from the operating business world. Of particular concern are the relationships among domestic and overseas markets, credit problems, and problems of access to critical production factors, including labor, technology, and energy.

Industry-specific production committees should be formed within the private sector to participate in the governmental consultative network. These committees may embrace not merely one industry but sets of linked industries having common concerns. They should include equal representation of labor and management. The committees should communicate regularly among themselves and periodically with government policymakers.

Many economists fear that sectoral policies, though they might conceivably be designed, will only founder on the shoals of intransigent labor-management confrontations. Some encouragement on the feasibility of labor-management cooperation may be taken from the country's worst crisis in local government, the virtual bankruptcy of New York City in 1975. Because reestablishing the city's credit rating depended on drastic cost reductions, union leaders representing local government employees played a pivotal role in preventing bankruptcy. Facing the brutal choice between massive layoffs, which would reduce membership, and reducing wages and benefits, they steered a difficult course between two evils. A relatively tight lid was kept on wage demands and fringe-benefit costs for five years. City workers adjusted to a substantial cut in real earnings, and even in 1980, with inflation at an all-time high, increases were kept below the maximum permitted by the national antiinflation guidelines and below the national median for industrial workers. The New York City experience—in which the unions also made substantial financial contributions directly by helping to refinance the city's debt with pension-fund purchases of new obligations—indicates that management and labor can jointly control costs and improve productivity in a crisis situation. Perhaps in the industrial sectors some of the cushions against economic adversity will have to be removed before the crisis is considered bad enough to draw forth similar cooperation.

Analytical Systems

The quality of policy decisions depends on the quality and timeliness of the information and analysis available to the decision-makers. Few governmental agencies have developed forward-looking, cross-functional, integrated analyses. The studies that do exist tend to be simplistic. For example, in December 1976, the comptroller general of the United States issued a report to the Congress entitled "Long Range Analysis Activities in Several Federal Agencies." This report was based on queries to seven agencies as to the nature and utilization of their long-range planning. The value of the activities was measured in quantitative terms, such as number of reports and number of personnel involved in analyses. The report, which unfortunately did not include recommendations, nevertheless concluded cogently:

> It is always tempting to look for organizational and structural devices to overcome difficulties encountered in activities such as long-range analyses. . . . Good long-range analyses can take place in a variety of organizational settings and it does not appear that choosing a particular structure

either assures good analysis or precludes it. Much more important is the existence of good communications and active involvement among those who are doing the analysis and those who are affected by it, along with the careful integration of the results of long-range analysis into the regular decision process of the agency.[5]

To date Congress has not recognized the salience of appropriate data systems boldly, and no administration has made structural information on the economy a top priority.

In a 1979 speech introducing a bill to promote American technological innovation, Senator Adlai Stevenson noted that in 1977 the Senate Committee on Commerce, Science and Transportation and the Subcommittee on Science Technology and Space had begun a review of industrial technology, but two years later they were unable to quantify or describe in an intellectually disciplined way the current status of American industrial technology and innovation. There is no need for such a situation to exist. The executive agencies and the nation's universities and research organizations are replete with industrial experts. The industrial trade associations annually produce reams of materials on markets, costs, and technology. The problem is not that information is unavailable; the problem is that no one is assigned the responsibility and the authority to gather and digest it in a policy-oriented framework.

In order to develop sectoral policies, existing data systems must be recast and new information systems must be established to illuminate the interrelated effects of major changes in resource availability and cost, market shifts, industrial organization, technology, and public policy on specific industries and sectors. A politically acceptable way to identify the industries to be included must be found. Once they are identified, both statistical and functional analyses are necessary. This implies that the role of industrial representatives must be greatly expanded and formalized.

Specific targets for an improved data collection and presentation system are

1. Assess the sectoral implications of international and domestic secular economic changes and distinguish them from short-term phenomena;
2. Assess the effects of public interventions on particular industries;
3. Determine the consequences of policy trade-offs—for example, between regulatory activities and development; and
4. Identify inflationary bottlenecks in key sectors in sufficient time to take mitigating action.

To reach these targets, data-collection and information agencies of the federal government must focus more on subnational industrial data. They must be given resources and a mandate to

1. Develop state product accounts;
2. Gather more detailed industrial capacity-utilization information than is presently available;
3. Generate employment data on a subnational level on an industry-specific basis; and
4. Generate capital-investment information on an industry-specific basis.

Fortunately, much of the needed information is available, but it is dispersed among many agencies. In many cases, improving the data base will require little additional expenditure. Costs can be cut by reducing overlap and duplication of data series. Many series are incompatible, thus precluding longitudinal, comparative, or geographical analysis. The quality of some series is poor, and if it cannot be improved at a reasonable cost, the series should be abandoned. An effective, authoritative data-management system whose priorities are set outside the individual data-gathering agencies would improve the quality and usefulness of statistical information.

Private-Sector Information

The private sector can be tapped much more effectively than it is now to provide basic information on production and markets. The analytic capability of industry specialists is an underutilized resource. Knowledge of industry structure and market potential, which only experienced private-sector practitioners have, can clarify choices. Ways should be found to regularize information flow from the private sector to government analysts. The private sector can be instrumental in seeing to it that government data series are relevant to real industry needs. Knowledgable persons in fields such as antitrust law, securities analysis, and investment banking should also be brought into the analytic process on a systematic basis.

Using Information

The sectoral-analysis staff of the federal government numbers more than 5,000 persons in the Department of Commerce, the Department of Transportation, the Department of Agriculture, the Bureau of Mines, the U.S. Treasury, the regulatory agencies, the Congress, the International Trade Commission, and the Office of the U.S. Trade Representative in the Executive Office of the President. These people conduct crisis studies, such as studies of the apparel industry or the auto-assembly industry, and prepare the valuable overviews published annually as the *Industrial Outlook*. They produce highly technical information on raw-materials availability. But their expertise is largely wasted because it lies in a policy vacuum. These experts are seldom asked the implications of their findings for policy. As a result, their evaluations of particular industries seldom indicate the consequences of government—or industry—taking one course of action or another.

Historical and current data are needed, of course. But they are inadequate guides to future choices. To anticipate, it is necessary to project trends that are likely to force change. It is necessary to define alternative scenarios. This necessarily involves some risk, as circumstances change often in a dynamic economy. However, much that will occur in the future, or at least the limits of the possible, can be foreseen. Informed scenario writing is the sine qua non of improved contingency planning. There are many possible actions to prevent the worst case from occurring, but neither government nor the private sector can act if they are not forewarned. By the same token, strategies to capture future opportunities will be more likely to succeed if they are planned well in advance and if they take into account all reasonable changes in circumstances.

Research Agenda

No matter which political party controls the White House and the Congress in the 1980s, it will be essential to develop well-thought-out strategies to improve the performance of American industry. The alternative is to continue patching up individual firms with economic Band-Aids. The opportunities to do this may become more frequent. The social bill, then, will soar. The productive sectors will have to produce more to provide the tax revenues to bail out the mismanaged firms or the losing industries. Lack of comprehensive, long-term sectoral policies can only contribute to more wrong decisions and retard the difficult choices that must be made. There is no time left to rationalize inaction with the false claim that "no one" can manage sectoral strategies.

Some difficult questions remain to be answered about some practical aspects of industrial policies. Answering them depends on carefully planned research. They must be answered on a sector-specific basis, for a few key sectors, before their implications for the entire economy can become clear.

First, what would be the effect of sector-specific fiscal policies or credit policies on capital markets? Is there any truth to the notion that sectoral policies would radically disrupt capital markets? What level of intervention on behalf of a specific sector could have such an outcome, if any? Would other sectors be "starved" for capital? Would the starved sectors, if any, be vital sectors? What relation do fiscal and monetary policies have to questions of allocating equity and debt through private markets? The federal government's obligation to use monetary and fiscal policy to manage sectors of the economy in the national interest is well established. Nevertheless, some solid research on the process of capital allocation to sectors is needed.

A murkier area of concern is antitrust law. What would be the necessary changes to existing law to conform to strategic sectoral objectives? In which sectors can economies of scale be encouraged without violating existing laws? For what sectors do legislative changes seem desirable? How can the opportunities for new innovative firms to start up and become profitable be made compatible with opportunities for whole national sectors to grow competitive internationally? For specific sectors, and perhaps for the economy as a whole, a review of antitrust statutes is needed that would gear regulation of monopoly and restrictive trade practices to international, rather than national, market conditions. The way to begin is on a sector-specific basis.

These are the major issues that now require attention. However, waiting for this research should not impede action. Although there are knowledge gaps, the nation is at a crossroad. Events will not wait for research. Thus we must proceed to gather the best information available, and get on with needed actions.

Administrative Reform

Administrative functions serve two primary purposes. One is to deliver programs to intended beneficiaries, and the other is to inform executives and legislators of pressing needs to modify policy. Much of the existing incoherence of federal interventions in the economy results from disorder in the administrative system. The system as it now functions cannot cope with the requirements of a comprehensive, development-oriented economic policy. It is geared to change programs, not policies or strategies. To facilitate timely decisions and streamline program delivery, some major changes will be needed.

The usual approach to this problem is to attempt major organizational reforms. However, the experience of the president's Reorganization Project, initiated in 1977, indicates that the obstacles to reorganization are virtually insurmountable in the short run. Vested institutional interests, plus external pressures, make it extremely difficult to transfer responsibilities from one agency to another.

Improving the federal administrative processes demands two simultaneous and coordinated efforts. One is an internal coordinating mechanism for each of the agencies now engaged in fiscal programs, regulatory programs, trade programs, area-development programs, and sectoral or industrial programs. The other is coordinating the actions of these agencies with one another. Counting all the data offices, as well as the program-delivery bureaus, there are at least 200 different units involved in these activities at present. Some can be consolidated or eliminated in the long run, but the recommended strategy focuses first on procedural rather than structural reform.

Time Management

Mismanagement of time is pervasive in both public and private institutions. It is the major cause of the excessive delay in the construction sector. It contributes to an unestimated and perhaps inestimable drain on our economy caused by inaction in other sectors. A homely example is the months and occasionally years of delay on the part of department stores and credit-card companies in correcting billing errors. Although on the one hand this reduces the labor productivity of the consumer, who must continually write letters trying to correct the error, the corporation bears costs as well, particularly since federal legislation allows consumers to withhold payments of disputed charges. Delay, whether caused by wrong action or by inaction, is a drain on the economy.

Much of the cost of mismanaged time is attributable to reluctance to make decisions. This can be eliminated through two kinds of remedies: automatic decision-making and better accountability.

Automatic decisions have been legislated by some governments. In New York City, for example, many proposals go into effect if no steps are taken to stop them within a specified time limit. Automatic decision-making should be extended to all levels of government for many kinds of approvals. It should be necessary to show cause why decision-making should be extended beyond the established time limits. Federal agencies and state and local government should be informed of the intent to extend a time limit for automatic decisions within a specified period; if the notification is not properly transmitted, then no extension of time should be permitted. Similarly, if agencies whose actions depend on previous action of another agency wish to extend the period of time within which they or the other agencies act, they should be required to request extension, and give reasons for it, well in advance. The administrative system should be biased toward action rather than toward inaction and delay.

The costs of any requested extension of the action time frame should be clearly indicated as a prerequisite for the extension. These costs should be calculated not merely on a current basis but over the life of the project or program. Inflation must be made an integral part of the cost model.

It is unrealistic to suppose that administrative agencies will take these steps without encouragement from the legislative branch. Congress should use its oversight responsibilities to require timely decisions and regular reports on the costs of delay. Moreover, congressional oversight can identify laws, regulations, and practices that contribute to delay, with a view to changing them.

To improve the intergovernmental management of time, beneficiaries of grants and other funding should be encouraged to improve management. Immediate funding for advancing projects as a reward for speedy implementation is one way to accomplish this.

Beneficiaries may also need some disincentives to delay. The most effective disincentive would be the threat to cancel grants and programs altogether if funds are not expended for the intended purpose within a particular time. This obviously raises some problems in terms of actual application: one would not halt construction on a partly completed public-works project because it was slow. But communities and agencies that have a poor track record could be given lower priority in the next round of funding.

Disputes as to who is at fault for delay will inevitably arise. Just as in the case of disputes over compliance with environmental regulations and health and product standards, the most efficient way to resolve these disputes would be to move toward mediation and away from litigation. The adversary procedures that were appropriate in a simple society are simply wasteful in a complex economy. As economists, we can not determine how the legal system should be altered to improve the economic efficiency of the society and enhance the social welfare of its members. But we can assert that, without changes in the system, legal wrangling over fault in administrative practices is bringing the system to a grinding halt faster than most people realize.

Coordinating Existing Development and Adjustment Assistance

Development-oriented sectoral policies will have increasingly significant geographic dimensions. Sectoral policies will serve area-development purposes by obviating the need for costly adjustment assistance in the long run. In the short run they will cushion the shock of transition, as industries and sectors change to meet changing economic circumstance.

For the immediate future, stronger, more effective links between sectoral and area-development programs can be forged. Improved coordination of the community and economic-development activities of the Economic Development Administration, the Farmers Home Administration, the Department of Housing and Urban Development Community Development Block Grant and Urban Development Action Grant, the

Small Business Administration, and the Regional Commissions is a must. These and other smaller units of the federal government provide almost $8 billion in development grants and credit assistance annually. They respond to the needs of different constituents. To determine where policy changes are indicated, the cumulative impact of these agencies' activities should be determined.

The potential effect of growth or decline in some sectors on the economic base of some cities and regions is very large. The news about this impact may not be pleasing. But government programs will not induce any change in the basic economic system unless they are addressed to the needs and possibilities of the system. Economic policy should deal with the economic base. Social policy should deal with the problems of people.

Evaluative Mechanisms

Government should assume the responsibility for evaluating the cumulative effect of all its interventions in the economy. But evaluation should be directed not to perpetuating programs but to adapting programs to meet changing circumstances, enhancing programs with high payoffs, and eliminating programs that are not contributing to a stronger economy. For each program, the outcomes to be measured and the measurement criteria have to be specified. For example, a loan program should be assessed in terms of its impact on the economic viability of the firm, not merely in terms of default or no-default on the loan.

Rebuilding the U.S. Economy

Sectoral policies should do two things: specify problems arising from and opportunities offered by structural economic change; and attempt to alleviate the problems and realize the opportunities offered by that change. Sectoral policies must operate between the macro and micro policy levels. They must be coordinated with macro policies and micro policies to ensure that policies at one level do not cancel out the effects of actions taken at another level.

The thrust of sectoral policy is to reduce frictions in the market system. These frictions arise from technological shifts, shifts in demand, shifts in market share, and different rates of maturation in the different sectors of the economy. These shifts take place gradually and unevenly over ups and downs of business cycles. Sectoral strategies must be aimed at the middle to long term, not at the short term.

Government and industry must abandon the adversary mode of policymaking that characterizes their relationship today. They must sit down together with the intention of coming to an understanding, if not an agreement. Together they must flag potential problems and real opportunities far enough in advance to do something about them. They must set up an information network based on what business leaders and labor leaders know and expect, not on statistics about what already happened.

A negotiated sectoral strategy will not be the same thing as consensus, although in some cases consensus may be achieved. Rather, a negotiated sectoral policy will be a bargain struck by all the interested parties. It will involve more than one industry, because the objective will be to facilitate the interindustry linkages, eliminate bottlenecks, and reduce uncertainties concerning supply and price of needed inputs at each major step along the productive chain. For example, the automobile-assembly corporations might assure a given level of demand for output of the machine-tool industry in exchange for quicker production of new tools. They might stretch out purchases beyond the period when they are needed to attract all the necessary production in the period they are most needed.

When government sits down with labor and business to understand the costs and consequences of various courses of action, it will be in a position to help industry, if necessary, to meet the objectives of improving productivity, expanding output and jobs, or expanding markets. But government participation can take many forms, ranging from not intervening at all in a particular industry to the other extreme of providing capital for specific uses. The nature and level of government involvement should be clearly related to specific benefits to be gained. Through the bargaining process, all parties—government, labor, and business—will gain a different perspective as they come to understand the trade-offs involved between specific costs and efficiency. Through the bargaining process, each party can commit itself to specific actions to reduce costs and increase efficiency. Over the long run, greater efficiency will lead to higher gross national product, and thus to the opportunity for greater equity in the distribution of income and improved quality of life.

The vehicle for this process should be industry production committees involving government, management, and labor on a parity basis. These committees would agree on objectives that would serve as the guide against which all existing and proposed public interventions in the economy would be evaluated. The committees would return recommendations to firms in their industry and linked industries on changes to increase productivity—whether they be new investment, new work rules, new product design, or others—and on market changes, including the policies of other governments and foreign competition. Had we had an automotive-sector policy five years ago, to accelerate production of advanced-design automobiles, government could have offered tax advantages for retiring obsolete tools and equipment. Management might have cut profit margins, and labor might have absorbed the costs of retraining and shutting down plants during retooling.

Models for such cooperative mechanisms exist. In World War II, American production took off like a rocket under the guidance of industry committees. More current examples exist on a modified scale, such as the Jamestown, New York, Labor Management Committee. Plant committees have achieved dramatic increases in output per manhour, quality control, and job satisfaction. These models can be adapted to an industry-specific context at the local level while, at the national level, sectorwide committees begin their job of sorting out scenarios.

Sectoral policy is not government planning in the sense that planning is applied in socialistic or mixed economies. We are not suggesting that government should decide what industry will produce. We are not suggesting that government should decide what wages labor should have, what hours should be worked, or what fringe benefits should be enjoyed by either labor or management. These decisions will remain the responsibilities of management and labor. But when taken in a cooperative mode and in the context of long-term objectives, the decisions should lead to greater economic stability and new growth opportunities.

Sectoral policy is not an industrial welfare program. It is not intended to shore up mismanaged firms. Assistance should be offered not to particular firms but rather to entire industries, with firms having the option to bargain to participate. This keeps open the option for viable firms in unstable industries to continue operation.

Moreover, if an industry appears to decline steadily despite reasonable attempts on the part of government, management, and labor to halt decline, there may well be good cause to phase out public interventions on its behalf. The estimated $150 billion or more in annual direct and indirect subsidies to private firms should produce some measurable economic change. Did the firm hire more people? Did it expand its markets or its product lines? Did it make enough incremental profit to finance substantial reinvestment, and, more importantly, did it reinvest? These should be the outcomes against which government's interventions are measured. The taxpaying public is entitled to tangible results from its contribution to rebuilding the economy.

Finally, sectoral policy is not a full-employment program. If it is successful, it will create long-term job opportunities. It will lead to opportunities for workers to retrain for new occupations when the inevitable shrinkage occurs in old occupations in certain industries. Although we have not dealt extensively with labor-mobility issues, it is important to note that both occupational and locational mobility have a strong impact on—and are, of course, affected by—secular change in the economy. Policies that create or eliminate demand for given skills in particular locations must be considered in the light of labor availability. At the same time, both older and younger workers may need to prepare for occupational change, perhaps several times during their working lives.

Sectoral policy is growth-oriented, not ameliorative. The overall goal is to increase productivity and expand markets. In many industries, this can only be accomplished by increasing automation and adding more capital for every unit of labor. There is no other way that long-term economic growth can be achieved. The alternative is to be satisfied with a no-growth economy—which means that there will be no opportunities to improve the standard of living, no further redistribution of income without political upheaval, and perhaps armed conflict. This alternative would be acceptable if it were inevitable. But it is not America's only choice.

Sectoral policy would, happily, eliminate some of the existing expensive and useless government apparatus. Many specific programs—in governmentese, "targeted" incentives—can be replaced by sectoral policy. Those targeted programs remaining can be made more effective and can be administered more efficiently.

Sectoral policy will aim to make market entry a possibility for all firms. It will assist all firms in a given industry to become competitive on an international scale. It will not set up artificial limits on type, size, location, or product character in order to measure out spoonfuls of federal aid at a very high cost per spoon. This approach may cause temporary dissatisfaction among some interest groups. But on balance it will improve the relations between government and the private sector, because it will base public-sector/private-sector interaction on mutual interest.

The nature of our political system is to be relatively unresponsive to changing circumstances until crisis forces action. The disadvantage of this system is that crisis-induced action may be shortsighted and incomplete. Its advantage is that emergencies tend to wipe away preconceived notions about what is and is not possible. Watershed shifts in relationships between the power centers in our society have generally occurred by changing institutions first and changing popular attitudes second.

Institutional change is not necessarily synonymous with new organization or new bureaucracies. All it requires is a new approach, new attitudes, new doors opened for discussion and compromise, and new lines of responsibility. The United States is on the edge of economic crisis. It is time for change.

Notes

1. U.S. Department of Commerce, unpublished data.
2. Ibid.

3. *New York Times,* March 3, 1980, p. D-10.

4. U.S. Steel Tripartite Advisory Committee, "Report of the Working Group on Modernization and Capital Formation," June 1980 (unpublished), p. 7.

5. U.S. Comptroller General, "Long Range Analysis Activities in Several Federal Agencies" (Washington, D.C.: U.S. Government Printing Office, December 1976), p. 48.

Bibliography

Academy for Contemporary Problems. *Regional Economic Development in the United States.* Background paper prepared for Working Party No. 6 of the Industry Committee, Organization for Economic Cooperation and Development, April 1979.

Academy for Contemporary Problems. *Revitalizing the Northeastern Economy: A Survey for Action.* Columbus, Ohio: The Academy for Contemporary Problems, 1977.

Academy for Contemporary Problems. *Stimulating the Economy of the Great Lakes States.* Columbus, Ohio: The Academy for Contemporary Problems, 1977.

Advisory Commission on Intergovernmental Relations. *Community Development: The Workings of a Federal-Local Block Grant.* Washington, D.C.: Advisory Commission on Intergovernmental Relations, March 1977.

Advisory Commission on Intergovernmental Relations. *Countercyclical Aid and Economic Stabilization.* Washington, D.C.: U.S. Government Printing Office, December 1978.

Advisory Commission on Intergovernmental Relations. *The Intergovernmental Grant System as Seen by Local, State, and Federal Officials.* Washington, D.C.: U.S. Government Printing Office, March 1977.

Allen, Kevin, ed. *Balanced National Growth.* Lexington, Mass.: Lexington Books, D.C. Heath, 1979.

Barnet, Richard J. *The Lean Years.* New York: Simon & Schuster, 1980.

Birch, David L. *The Job Generation Process.* Paper prepared for the U.S. Dept. of Commerce. Cambridge: Massachusetts Institute of Technology, Program on Neighborhood and Regional Change, 1979 (mimeographed).

Bivens, W.E., III, and Marinich, Joseph S. *State Departments of Community and Economic Development: Frameworks for Coordinating Implementation.* Washington, D.C.: Council of State Community Affairs Agencies, June 1978.

Bowen, William. "Better Prospects for our Ailing Productivity, The U.S. Economy in the '80s." *Fortune,* December 3, 1979.

"Can Semiconductors Survive Big Business?" *Business Week,* December 3, 1980.

Choate, Pat. *As Time Goes By: The Costs and Consequences of Delay* Columbus, Ohio: Academy for Contemporary Problems, June 1980.

Choate, Pat. "The Great American Delay" (an Editorial). *The Washington Post,* July 6, 1980.

Clawson, Marion. *New Deal Planning: The National Resources Planning Board.* Washington, D.C.: Resources for the Future, October 1979.

Cohen, Robert B. "Economic Crisis, National Industrial Strategies and Multi-National Corporations." Paper prepared for the annual meeting of the American Political Science Association, Washington, D.C., September 2, 1979 (mimeographed).

Cohen, Robert B. *The Impact of Foreign Direct Investment on U.S. Cities and Regions.* Prepared for U.S. Department of Housing and Urban Development. Arlington, Va.: The Analytic Sciences Corporation, February 1979.

Cohen, Robert B. "Progress Report: Research into the Service Economy at the Corporate Level." New York: Columbia University, September 1979 (mimeographed).

Commission of the European Communities. *European Economic and Monetary Union.* Brussels: Commission of the European Communities, March 1979.

Commission of the European Communities. *The European Monetary System.* Brussels: Commission of the European Communities, April 1979.

Commission of the European Communities. *Report of the Study Group on the Role of Public Finance in European Integration; Volume II: Individual Contributions and Working Papers.* Brussels: Commission of the European Communities, April 1977.

Committee for Economic Development. *Stimulating Technological Progress.* New York: Committee for Economic Development, January 1980.

Cornman, John M., and Madden, J. Patrick. *The Essential Process for a Successful Rural Strategy.* Washington, D.C.: National Rural Center, December 1977.

Council for Northeast Economic Action. *The 1977 Clean Air Act Amendments: The Impact on Northeastern Business.* Boston: Council for Northeast Economic Action, April 1979.

Daniels, Belden, and Kieschnick, Michael. "MBE Capital Markets: An Analysis of Empirical Data, Current Federal Intervention and Proposed Innovations." Washington, D.C.: Council of State Planning Agencies, September 1978.

Davis, John. *Technology for a Changing World.* London: Intermediate Technology Publications Ltd, 1978.

Economic Consulting Services, Inc. *Impact of Import Penetration on Labor in Selected U.S. Industries and Related Problems of Adjustment.* Paper prepared for the Conference on the Employment Effects of International Trade, sponsored by U.S. Department of Labor and National Commission for Manpower Policy, Washington, D.C., November 15, 1978.

Feaver, Douglas. "DOT Chief Says Ports Need Better Road, Rail Access." *The Washington Post,* November 9, 1979.

Forrester, Jay W. "Changing Economic Patterns," *Technology Review* 80: 8 (August/September 1978).

Franko, Lawrence G. *Industrial Policy in Europe: Solution or Problem?* July 1978 (draft).

Garn, Harvey A., et al. *Environmental Policies and Economic Development.* Washington, D.C.: The Urban Institute, February 1979.

Garnick, Daniel. "The Regional Statistics System." Paper prepared for the Conference on Modeling the Multi-Region Economic System: Perspectives for the Eighties, Philadelphia, Pennsylvania, June 14-15, 1979.

Garnick, Daniel, and Renshaw, Vernon. "Competing Hypotheses on the Outlook for Cities and Regions: What the Data Reveal and Conceal." Paper prepared for the North American Meetings of the Regional Science Association, Los Angeles, California, November 9-11, 1979.

German Information Center. *Co-determination: Worker Participation in German Industry.* New York: German Information Center.

Gustely, Richard D. *Measuring the Regional Economic Impacts of Federal Grant Programs.* Washington, D.C.: U.S. Department of Commerce, June 15, 1978 (draft).

Haffner, Bernard. *The Potential Economic Impact of U.S. Regulations on the Copper Industry.* Washington, D.C.: U.S. Department of Commerce, April 1979 (mimeographed).

Hoffman, Cary, and Shapero, Albert. *Providing the Industrial Ecology Required for the Survival and Growth of Small Technical Companies.* Austin, Texas: Multi-Disciplinary Research, Inc., May 1971.

Javits, Jacob K. "New Directions for Savings and Investments in 1980." *Journal of the Institute for Socioeconomic Studies* 4, No. 4 (Winter 1979): 1.

Jorgenson, Dale W. "Energy and the Future U.S. Economy." *The Wharton Magazine* 3, no. 4 (Summer 1979): 15.

Kaiser Aluminum and Chemical Corporation. *1978 Annual Report.* Oakland, Calif.

Keyserling, Leon H. *Full Employment Without Inflation.* Washington, D.C.: Conference on Economic Progress, January 1975.

Liu, Ben-chieh. "Costs of Air Pollution and Benefits of Its Control." *American Journal of Economics and Sociology* 38, no. 2 (April 1979): 187.

Liu, Ben-chieh. "Differential Net Migration Rates and the Quality of Life." *Review of Economics and Statistics* 57, no. 3 (August 1975): 329.

Liu, Ben-chieh. "Quality of Life: Concept, Measures and Results." *American Journal of Economics and Sociology* 34, no. 1 (January 1975): 1.

Liu, Ben-chieh. "Technological Change and Environmental Quality: A Preliminary Survey of Environmental Indicators in Medium Metropolitan Areas." *Technological Forecasting and Social Change* 12 (1978): 325.

Massey, Doreen B., and Meegan, Richard A. "Industrial Restructuring versus the Cities." *Urban Studies* (1978).

Meadows, George Richard, and Mitrisin, John. *A National Development Bank: Survey and Discussion of the Literature on Capital Shortages and Employment Changes in Distressed Areas.* Washington, D.C.: Library of Congress, Congressional Research Service, April 1979.

Meanley, Carolyn A., ed. *Productivity Perspectives.* Houston: American Productivity Center, 1980.

National Science Foundation, Office of Exploratory Research and Problem Assessment, Research Applications Directorate. *Candidates and Priorities for Technology Assessments: Volume IV; An Approach to Priorities.* Washington, D.C.: National Science Foundation, March 1973.

"The OPEC Decade." *The Economist* (December 29, 1979): 39.

Organization for Economic Cooperation and Development. *Indicators of Industrial Activity.* Paris: OECD, 1979.

Organization for Economic Cooperation and Development. *Policies for Promoting Industrial Adaptation.* Paris: OECD, 1976.

Putnam, Hayes & Bartlett, Inc. *Economics of International Steel Trade: Policy Implications for the United States.* Newton, Mass.: Putnam, Hayes & Bartlett, Inc., May 1977.

Rohatyn, Felix G. "Do What F.D.R. Did." *The New York Times,* October 3, 1979.

Rosenblatt, Samuel M. "Trade Adjustment Assistance Programs: Crossroads or Dead End? *Law and Policy in International Business* 9, no. 4 (1978): 1065.

Ruttenberg, Friedman, Kilgallon, Gutchess and Associates. *The Impact of Manufacturing Trade on Employment.* Prepared for the Conference on the Employment Effects of International Trade, Washington, D.C., November 15, 1978.

Schwartz, Gail Garfield. *Bridges to the Future: Forces Impacting Urban Economies.* Columbus, Ohio: Academy for Contemporary Problems, May 1978.

Schwartz, Gail Garfield. *Retrospect and Prospects: An Urban Policy Profile of the United States.* Columbus, Ohio: Academy for Contemporary Problems; April 1979.

Schwartz, Gail Garfield. *Urban Economic Development in Great Britain and West Germany: Lessons for the United States.* Columbus, Ohio: Academy for Contemporary Problems, 1980.

Schwartz, Gail Garfield, and Choate, Pat. *Revitalizing the U.S. Economy:*

A Brief for National Sectoral Policies. Columbus, Ohio: Academy for Contemporary Problems, January 1980.

Smith, Steve. *Testimony on the National Public Works and Economic Development Act of 1979 to the Regional and Community Development Subcommittee of the Senate Environment and Public Works Committee.* Washington, D.C.: Council of State Planning Agencies, 1979.

Steel Tripartite Advisory Committee. Unpublished Proceedings. Washington, D.C., June 18, 1980.

Stokes, Henry Scott. "Japan's Goal: Lead in Computers." *The New York Times,* December 12, 1979.

The Sun Belt. Articles selected from *The Plain Dealer,* September 16 to September 24, 1979. Cleveland, Ohio: Plain Dealer Publishing Co., 1979.

Tropper, Peter, and Abrams, Amy. "The Regional Impact of The Crisis at Chrysler." Washington, D.C.: Northeast-Midwest Institute, December 1979.

United Kingdom, Chancellor of the Exchequer. *The Nationalized Industries.* London: Her Majesty's Stationery Office, March 1978.

United Kingdom, Department of Industry. *Incentives for Industry in the Areas for Expansion.* London: Her Majesty's Stationery Office, September 1979.

U.S., Congress, Congressional Budget Office. *Economic Conversion: What Should Be the Government's Role?* Washington, D.C.: U.S. Government Printing Office, January 1980.

U.S., Congress, Congressional Budget Office. *The U.S. Balance of International Payments and the U.S. Economy: Developments in 1978 and Early 1979.* Washington, D.C.: U.S. Government Printing Office, November 1979.

U.S., Congress, Congressional Budget Office. *U.S. Raw Materials Policy: Problems and Possible Solutions.* Washington, D.C.: U.S. Government Printing Office, December 28, 1976.

U.S., Congress, House of Representatives, Committee on Education and Labor. *Full Employment and Balanced Growth Act of 1977.* Hearing before the Subcommittee on Employment Opportunities, June 22, 1977. Washington, D.C.: U.S. Government Printing Office.

U.S., Congress, House of Representatives, Committee on Education and Labor. *The Full Employment and Balanced Growth Act of 1977; Authorization of Appropriations for CETA, and the President's Economic Stimulus Proposals.* Hearings before the Subcommittee on Employment Opportunities, Vol. 2; February 22, February 24, March 2, March 16, 1977. Washington, D.C.: U.S. Government Printing Office.

U.S., Congress, House of Representatives, Committee on Education and

Labor. *Hearings before the Subcommittee on Employment Opportunities,* January 18 and 19, 1978. Washington, D.C.: U.S. Government Printing Office.

U.S., Congress, House of Representatives, Committee on Education and Labor. *Oversight Hearings on the Full Employment and Balanced Growth Act of 1978.* Hearings before the Subcommittee on Employment Opportunities, February 13 and 14, 1979. Washington, D.C.: U.S. Government Printing Office.

U.S., Congress, House of Representatives, Committee on Small Business. *Future of Small Business in America.* Washington, D.C.: U.S. Government Printing Office, August 1979.

U.S., Congress, House of Representatives, Committee on Small Business, Subcommittee on Antitrust, Consumers and Employment. *Future of Small Business in America.* Washington, D.C.: U.S. Government Printing Office, 1978.

U.S., Congress, Joint Economic Committee. *Anticipating Disruptive Imports.* Washington, D.C.: U.S. Government Printing Office, 1978.

U.S., Congress, Joint Economic Committee. *Capital Formation.* Washington, D.C.: U.S. Government Printing Office, 1977.

U.S., Congress, Joint Economic Committee. *The Economics of Federal Subsidy Programs; Part 2—International Subsidies.* Washington, D.C.: U.S. Government Printing Office, 1972.

U.S., Congress, Joint Economic Committee. *Federal Subsidy Programs.* Staff study prepared for the Subcommittee on Priorities and Economy in Government. Washington, D.C.: U.S. Government Printing Office, 1974.

U.S., Congress, Joint Economic Committee. *The Trade Deficit: How Much of a Problem? What Remedy?* Hearing before the Subcommittee on International Economics, October 11, 1977. Washington, D.C.: U.S. Government Printing Office.

U.S., Congress, Joint Economic Committee, Subcommittee on Economic Growth. *Technology, Economic Growth, and International Competitiveness.* Washington, D.C.: U.S. Government Printing Office, 1975.

U.S., Congress, Joint Economic Committee, Subcommittee on Economic Growth and Stabilization. *The Cost of Government Regulation.* Washington, D.C.: U.S. Government Printing Office, 1978.

U.S., Congress, Joint Economic Committee, Subcommittee on Economic Growth and Stabilization. *The Costs of Governmental Regulation of Business.* Washington, D.C.: U.S. Government Office, 1978.

U.S., Congress, Joint Economic Committee, Subcommittee on Economic Growth and Stabilization. *Deteriorating Infrastructure in Urban and Rural Areas.* Washington, D.C.: U.S. Government Printing Office, 1979.

U.S., Congress, Joint Economic Committee, Subcommittee on Economic

Growth and Stabilization. *The Role of Federal Tax Policy in Stimulating Capital Formation and Economic Growth.* Washington, D.C.: U.S. Government Printing Office, 1978.

U.S., Congress, Joint Economic Committee, Subcommittee on Fiscal and Intergovernmental Policy. *Central City Businesses—Plans and Problems.* Washington, D.C.: U.S. Government Printing Office, 1979.

U.S., Congress, Joint Economic Committee, Subcommittee on Fiscal and Intergovernmental Policy. *Regional Impact of Current Recession.* Washington, D.C.: U.S. Government Printing Office, 1980.

U.S., Congress, Joint Economic Committee, Subcommittee on Priorities and Economy in Government. *The Economics of Federal Subsidy Programs. Part 8—Selected Subsidies.* Washington, D.C.: U.S. Government Printing Office, 1974.

U.S., Congress, Joint Economic Committee, Subcommittee on Priorities and Economy in Government. *Federal Subsidy Programs.* Washington, D.C.: U.S. Government Printing Office, 1974.

U.S., Congress, Office of Technology Assessment. *Anticipating the Impacts of Legislation.* Washington, D.C.: Office of Technology Assessment, June 1979.

U.S., Congress, Office of Technology Assessment. *Government Involvement in the Innovation Process.* Washington, D.C.: U.S. Government Printing Office, 1978.

U.S., Congress, Senate, Committee on Banking, Housing and Urban Affairs. *Multilateral Trade Negotiations.* Hearings before the Subcommittee on International Finance, April 4 and 5, 1979. Washington, D.C.: U.S. Government Printing Office.

U.S., Congress, Senate, Committee on Commerce, Science, and Transportation. *Oversight on the Office of Science and Technology Policy.* Hearings before the Subcommittee on Science, Technology, and Space, March 7 and 21, 1979; Washington, D.C.: U.S. Government Printing Office.

U.S., Congress, Senate, Committee on Governmental Affairs. *Reorganization Plan No. 1 of 1977.* Washington, D.C.: U.S. Government Printing Office, 1977.

U.S., Congress, Senate, Committee on Governmental Affairs. *Reorganization Plan No. 2 of 1977.* Washington, D.C.: U.S. Government Printing Office, 1977.

U.S., Department of Commerce. *Air and Water Purification and Pollution Control Equipment.* Washington, D.C.: U.S. Government Printing Office, April 1976.

U.S., Department of Commerce. *Factors Affecting the International Transfer of Technology Among Developed Countries.* Washington, D.C.: U.S. Government Printing Office, February 1970.

U.S., Department of Commerce, Advisory Committee on Industrial Innovation. *The Effects of Domestic Policies of the Federal Government Upon Innovation by Small Businesses.* Washington, D.C.: U.S. Department of Commerce, May 1979.

U.S., Department of Commerce, Advisory Committee on Industrial Innovation, Subcommittee on Economic and Trade Policy. *Draft Report on Economic and Trade Policy.* Springfield, Va.: National Technical Information Service, December 20, 1978.

U.S., Department of Commerce, Advisory Committee on Industrial Innovation, Subcommittee on Labor. *A Statement of the Labor Advisory Subcommittee on Industrial Innovation.* Springfield, Va.: National Technical Information Service, December 1978.

U.S., Department of Commerce, Advisory Committee on Industrial Innovation, Subcommittee on Procurement and Direct Support of Research and Development. *Draft Report on Federal Procurement Policy.* Washington, D.C.: U.S. Department of Commerce, December 1978.

U.S., Department of Commerce, Advisory Committee on Industrial Innovation, Subcommittee on Regulation of Industry Structure and Competition. *Draft Report on Regulation of Industry Structure and Competition.* Washington, D.C.: U.S. Department of Commerce, December 1978.

U.S., Department of Commerce, Bureau of the Census. *Regional Organizations: 1977 Census of Governments.* Washington, D.C.: U.S. Government Printing Office, August 1978.

U.S., Department of Commerce, Bureau of the Census, *Statistical Abstract of the United States: 1979* (100th edition) Washington, D.C.: U.S. Government Printing Office, 1979.

U.S., Department of Commerce, Bureau of Economic Analysis. *Business Statistics/1977.* Washington, D.C.: U.S. Government Printing Office, March 1978.

U.S., Department of Commerce, Domestic and International Business Administration. *Materials on Practical Aspects of Exporting, International Licensing and Investing.* Washington, D.C.: U.S. Government Printing Office, November 1975.

U.S., Department of Commerce, Domestic and International Business Administration, Bureau of Domestic Commerce. *The American Computer Industry in its International Competitive Environment.* Washington, D.C.: U.S. Government Printing Office, November 1976.

U.S., Department of Commerce, Domestic and International Business Administration, Bureau of Domestic Commerce. *The Impact of Electronics on the U.S. Calculator Industry: 1965-1974.* Washington, D.C.: U.S. Government Printing Office, 1975.

U.S., Department of Commerce, Domestic and International Business Administration, Bureau of Domestic Commerce, *Study of the Expected*

Impact on the Forest Products Industries of Assumed Nationwide Application of the Monongahela-Tongass Court Decisions. Staff study, August 1976.

U.S., Department of Commerce, Domestic and International Business Administration, Bureau of Domestic Commerce. *The U.S. Consumer Electronics Industry.* Washington, D.C.: U.S. Government Printing Office, September 1975.

U.S., Department of Commerce, Economic Development Administration. *The Development of a Subnational Economic Development Policy.* September 1977 (mimeographed).

U.S., Department of Commerce, Economic Development Administration. *Human Resources and Regional Economic Development.* Edited by Paul V. Braden. Washington, D.C.: U.S. Government Printing Office, October 1977.

U.S., Department of Commerce, Economic Development Administration. *Jobs Through Economic Development.* Washington, D.C.: U.S. Department of Commerce, 1979.

U.S., Department of Commerce,, Industry and Trade Administration. *Copper: Quarterly Report.* Washington, D.C.: U.S. Government Printing Office, Winter 1978–1979.

U.S., Department of Commerce, Industry and Trade Administration. *Measuring Markets: A Guide to the Use of Federal and State Statistical Data.* Washington, D.C.: U.S. Government Printing Office, August 1979.

U.S., Department of Commerce, Industry and Trade Administration. *The Motor Vehicle Leasing and Rental Industry: Trends and Prospects.* Washington, D.C.: U.S. Government Printing Office, 1979.

U.S., Department of Commerce, Industry and Trade Administration. *The Potential Economic Impact of U.S. Regulations on the U.S. Copper Industry.* Washington, D.C., U.S. Department of Commerce, April 1979.

U.S., Department of Commerce, Industry and Trade Administration. *A Report on the U.S. Semiconductor Industry.* Washington, D.C.: U.S. Government Printing Office, September 1979.

U.S., Department of Commerce, Industry and Trade Administration. *U.S. Export Opportunities in Japan.* Washington, D.C.: U.S. Government Printing Office, August 1978.

U.S., Department of Commerce, Industry and Trade Administration. *1980 U.S. Industrial Outlook.* Washington, D.C.: U.S. Government Printing Office, January 1980.

U.S., Department of Commerce, Office of Business Research and Analysis. *Impact of Environmental, Energy, and Safety Regulations and of Emerging Market Factors upon the United States Sector of the North*

American Automotive Industry. Washington, D.C.: National Technical Information Service (PB-278 991), August 1977.

U.S., Department of Commerce, Patent and Trademark Office. *Technology Assessment and Forecast.* Washington, D.C.: U.S. Government Printing Office, 1979.

U.S., Department of Housing and Urban Development. *Developmental Needs of Small Cities.* Washington, D.C.: U.S. Government Printing Office, 1979.

U.S., Department of Housing and Urban Development. *The President's 1978 National Urban Policy Report.* Washington, D.C.: U.S. Government Printing Office, August 1978.

U.S., Department of Housing and Urban Development, Office of Evaluation, Community Planning and Development. *Urban Development Action Grant Program: First Annual Report.* Washington, D.C.: U.S. Government Printing Office, June 1979.

U.S., Department of Housing and Urban Development, Office of Policy Development and Research. *State Planning: Intergovernmental Policy Coordination.* Washington, D.C.: U.S. Government Printing Office, August 1976.

U.S. Department of Justice, Antitrust Division. *Antitrust Guide for International Operations.* Washington, D.C.: U.S. Government Printing Office, March 1977.

U.S., Department of Labor, Bureau of Labor Statistics. *Productivity and the Economy.* Washington, D.C.: U.S. Government Printing Office, 1977.

U.S., Department of Labor, Bureau of Labor Statistics. *The Structure of the U.S. Economy in 1980 and 1985.* Washington, D.C.: U.S. Government Printing Office, 1975.

U.S., Department of the Treasury. *Federal Aid to States; Fiscal Year 1978.* Washington, D.C., U.S. Government Printing Office, 1978.

U.S., Executive Office of the President. *Economic Report of the President.* Washington, D.C., U.S. Government Printing Office, 1980.

U.S., Executive Office of the President. *Executive Order 12188: International Trade Functions.* January 1980.

U.S., Executive Office of the President, Council on International Economic Policy. *International Economic Report of the President.* Washington, D.C.: U.S. Government Printing Office, January 1977.

U.S., Executive Office of the President, Council on Wage and Price Stability. *Report to the President on Prices and Costs in the United States Steel Industry.* Washington, D.C.: U.S. Government Printing Office, October 1977.

U.S., Executive Office of the President, Office of Management and Budget. *Federal Credit Programs.* Washington, D.C.: Office of Management and Budget, January 1979.

U.S., Executive Office of the President, Office of Management and Budget. *Organizing For Development: The Final Report of the Reorganization Study of Federal Community and Economic Development Programs.* Washington, D.C.: Office of Management and Budget, January 1979.

U.S., Executive Office of the President, Office of Management and Budget. "Report to Congress: Implementation of the Joint Funding Simplification Act of 1974 (Public Law 93-510)." February 1979 (mimeographed).

U.S., Executive Office of the President, Office of Management and Budget, President's Reorganization Project. *Reorganization Study of Local Development Assistance Programs.* Washington, D.C.: Office of Management and Budget, December 1978.

U.S., Executive Office of the President, Office of Management and Budget, Special Studies Division, Economics and Government. *Public Works as Countercyclical Assistance.* November 1979.

U.S., General Accounting Office. *Manufacturng Technology—A Changing Challenge to Improved Productivity.* Report to the Congress by the Comptroller General, Washington, D.C., June 3, 1976.

U.S., General Accounting Office. *Report to the Congress by the Comptroller General of the United States; Learning to Look Ahead: The Need for a National Materials Policy and Planning Process.* Washington, D.C. U.S. Government Printing Office, 1976.

U.S., Office of the White House Press Secretary. "Fact Sheet: The President's Industrial Innovation Initiatives." Washington, D.C.: The White House, October 31, 1979 (mimeographed).

U.S., Office of the White House Press Secretary. "Remarks of the President on Innovation Initiatives." Washington, D.C.: The White House, October 31, 1979.

U.S., White House. *A New Partnership to Conserve America's Communities.* Washington, D.C.: U.S. Government Printing Office, June 1979.

U.S., White House. *Small Community and Rural Development Policy.* December 20, 1979.

U.S., White House Conference on the Industrial World Ahead. *A Look at Business in 1990.* Washington, D.C.: U.S. Government Printing Office, 1972.

van Ypersele de Strihou, Jacques. *Operating Principles and Procedures of the European Monetary System.* Washington, D.C.: Brookings Institution. Paper prepared for Seminar on the European Monetary System, April 18–19, 1979.

Vehorn, Charles L. *The Regional Distribution of Federal Grants-in-Aid.* Columbus, Ohio: Academy for Contemporary Problems, November 1977.

Vernez, Georges, and Vaughan, Roger. *Assessment of Countercyclical*

Public Works and Public Service Employment Programs. Santa
    Monica: Rand Corporation, September 1978.
Vernez, Georges, Vaughan, Roger, Burright, Burke, and Coleman, Sin-
    clair. *Regional Cycles and Employment Effects of Public Works
    Investments.* Santa Monica: Rand Corporation, January 1977.
Vogel, Ezra F. "Guided Free Enterprise in Japan." *Harvard Business
    Review* (May-June 1978): 162.
Vogel, Ezra F. *Japan as Number One: Lessons for America.* Cambridge,
    Mass.: Harvard University Press, 1969.
Weisz, Morris. *Strategies for Adjustment Assistance: Experience in the
    U.S. and Abroad and Implications for Future U.S. Programs.* Confer-
    ence on the Employment Effects of International Trade. Bureau of
    International Labor Affairs, U.S. Department of Labor. Washington,
    D.C., November 15, 1979 (mimeographed).
Widner, Ralph R. "Regional Research and Regional Policy in the United
    States." Paper prepared for the Seminar on the Relationship between
    Research and Regional Policy, Organization for Economic Coopera-
    tion and Development, Paris, France, November 8-9, 1979.
Weidenbaum, Murray. *Business, Government, and the Public* (Er﹍ewood
    Cliffs, N.J.: Prentice-Hall, Inc., 1977).

Index

Administrative reform, U.S. government, 106-9
Advertising, 62-63; vital statistics, 62
Advertising Age, 62
AFL-CIO, 40
Africa, 49
Alabama, 38, 55, 79
Aluminum industry, 50, 53-55
American Motors, 31
American Productivity Center, 85
American Telephone and Telegraph, 44
Antitrust, 1, 60, 75-76, 104, 106
Apparel industry, 40, 50, 55-56; vital statistics, 55
Area-development policy, 76-82
Area Redevelopment Act, 1961, 76-77
Arkansas, 55
Arrangement Regarding International Trade in Textiles, 56
Asia, 6
Automation, 5, 93
Automobile industry, 4, 40, 79-81, 90-95
Automotive sector, 90-94, 110
Australia, 49, 55

Balance of payments, U.S., 32
Balance of trade, international, 32-40
Bank of Japan, 41-42
Barnet, Richard, 43-44
Bauxite, 54-55; alternatives to, 55
Biochemicals, biochemistry, 3, 28, 50, 58-60
Brazil, 49
Bureau of Mines, U.S., 55, 104

California, 56, 79
Canada: GDP, 14, 15t; productivity growth rate, 17; R&D, 25; trade policy, 74, 79
Capacity utilization, 70
Capital Cost Recover Act (Jones-Conable Bill), 68-70

Capital Formation Group, (Steel Tripartite Advisory Committee), 96
Capital investment, 19-22, 89, 95, 104, 105; diversion, effects on GNP, 20; formation, 95-96; nonresidential, as percentage of GNP, 21; productivity and, 85
Capital stock, maturation of, 22
Cartelization, international, 44
Central America, 6
Chicago, 86
Chromite, 49
Chromium, 38, 49-50
Chrysler Corporation, 4, 31, 44, 45, 67, 80, 90, 92
Clayton Act, 1914, 75
Cobalt, 38
Commerce in Labor Adjustment Action Committee, 96
Common Market. *See* Organization for Economic Cooperation and Development
Community Development Block Grant program, 79, 86
Congress, U.S., 4, 60, 72, 86, 98, 100, 102, 103, 104, 107
Congressional Budget Office, 49
Construction delay, 85-87
Consultative system; government, 100-101; private sector, 101-102
Consumer protection, 87
Consumer spending, 14
Copper: industry, regulatory actions and, 84-85; market, 44
Corporations, government support of, 45. *See also individual corporations by name*
Corporations, nonfinancial, output and stocks, 23
Council of Economic Advisors, 100
Council on Wage and Price Stability, 9, 52

127

About the Authors

Gail Garfield Schwartz is a Senior Fellow of the Academy for Contemporary Problems, Washington, D.C. The Academy is a public-policy research center established by seven national associations of state and local government. Dr. Schwartz directed the Division of Economic Planning and Development of the New York City Planning Commission for several years, and in that capacity she designed and implemented sectoral strategies. She led the 1976 task force that developed New York City's five-year economic-recovery program. Her earlier experience included research at Columbia University and private consulting.

Dr. Schwartz is the author of many papers on urban issues and economic policy and is completing two books on urban change in the United States and Europe for Lexington Books. She received the doctorate from Columbia University and in 1976–1977 was a Loeb Fellow in Advanced Environmental Science at Harvard.

Pat Choate is a Visiting Federal Fellow at the Academy for Contemporary Problems, Washington, D.C., where he has made a special study of the construction sector and is working on a book dealing with public-investment strategies. He received the Ph.D. in economics from the University of Oklahoma. A specialist in the intra- and inter-governmental aspects of economic development, Dr. Choate served as a senior staff member of the President's Reorganization Project in 1978–1979. His wide experience in government includes several positions with the Economic Development Administration in the U.S. Department of Commerce, where he served as director of the Office of Economic Research and as regional director for the Southern Region and Appalachia. He was also commissioner of economic and community development for the state of Tennessee and director of state planning in Oklahoma.